Inspiring and heroic li

SAINTS AND
SAINTLY PEOPLE

saints and saintly peopl

Clare Richards
Illustrated by Donald Melvin

kevin
mayhew

First published in 2003 by

KEVIN MAYHEW LTD
Buxhall, Stowmarket, Suffolk, IP14 3BW
E-mail: info@kevinmayhewltd.com

KINGSGATE PUBLISHING INC
1000 Pannell Street, Suite G, Columbia, MO 65201
E-mail: sales@kingsgatepublishing.com

9 8 7 6 5 4 3 2 1 0

ISBN 1 84417 093 4
Catalogue No 1500599

Cover design by Angela Selfe
Edited by Peter Edwards
Typeset by Louise Selfe

Printed and bound in Great Britain

CONTENTS

INTRODUCTION

This is my second book about saints. In the first one, *Saints are Great* (also published as *Extraordinary Ordinary People*), I wrote about the better-known saints like St Francis of Assisi and St Brigid. In this volume I am introducing lesser-known saints and saintly people. It is obvious to me, after researching the lives of these heroic men and women, that saints are ordinary people like us. What makes them extraordinary is that they do rather better than most of us at following the example of Jesus.

In this book I am bearing in mind that St Paul addressed all followers of Jesus as 'saints'. He expected all Christians to be serious about living their lives according to the Gospel – compassionate, self-sacrificing and generous. The Roman Catholic Church and the Orthodox Church publicly proclaim their saints. They officially recognise (canonise) them as people whose lives were so full of holiness that the Church can declare them to be in heaven.

I have included in this volume some of these canonised saints, but also many others who are simply recognised by the Anglican Church and commemorated in their liturgy. I have also included saintly people from other Christian denominations, and a few from other world religions. Goodness is not a Christian preserve.

To complete the picture I have included examples of saintly people who are alive now, who offer us examples of holiness in the rather less than holy world of the twenty-first century. I hope the children who read the book will become aware that saints aren't impossible 'goody-goodies', but happy people who realise that happiness usually comes alongside generosity. Saints and saintly people don't need to be perfect. They are people slowly growing towards perfection. They make mistakes as we all do. They are sometimes horribly impossible, as we all are. But they are remembered for the good they bring to others, and the love that shines through their very ordinary lives.

As in my first book these short biographies are beautifully illustrated by Donald Melvin, who is able to put the 'saints' into their historical and geographical context.

REFLECTIONS

ANNE MARY TAIGI (BLESSED)

B. 1769

FEAST DAY: 9 JUNE

BEATIFIED IN 1920

How many arguments have you had with your brothers and sisters, or with your parents this week? The one thing that all families share is the ability to have good squabbles! It is a sad fact that squabbles can be turned into angry rows, and sometimes they are bad enough to break up the family. Anne Mary Taigi's family could easily have fallen apart because her husband, Domenico, had a violent temper that upset the family over and over again. But Anne was patient and loving. She found a way to bring harmony and peace to her family, friends and neighbours. For this reason the Catholic Church chose to call her 'Blessed'.

Anne Mary was born in Italy into a poor family and left home to become a servant. When she was 21 years old she married Domenico Taigi. He was a servant in the Chigi Palace in Rome. They had seven children, but only five survived childbirth. The couple never had much money and perhaps this led to Domenico's bad moods. Anne managed to keep the family fed and healthy in spite of difficult times. Her own parents were awkward and demanding; one daughter-in-law was downright unpleasant. Yet she took them into her home when they needed help. Later, when a daughter was widowed she took her and her six children back home too.

The extraordinary thing about this mother was that she always seemed cheerful and welcoming. The home was often full of visitors who came to ask her advice or for practical aid. Anne could always find ways to help those worse off than herself. How did she find the strength to do this? Early in her marriage she became convinced that God was close to her and she began to put aside time for prayer. She went to daily morning Mass and ended the day with the rosary and a reading from the lives of the saints.

When she died in 1837 Domenico told everyone that he had been an impatient and moody husband to a saintly wife. He spoke of her goodness and gentle patience and her welcoming smile for everyone. He was amazed that she had kept their large, argumentative family together. He said, 'I believe that God has received her into heaven because of her great virtue. And I hope that she will pray for me and our family.'

The Church thought it would be helpful for all families, especially mothers, to learn from her example. That is why she is now honoured as a saint, and remembered on 9 June.

THINK ABOUT IT
How can you make life much easier for your family this coming weekend?

Anne Mary Taigi

ANNE MARY TAIGI
BORN 1769
DIED 1837

Anthony Ashley Cooper

ANTHONY ASHLEY COOPER   B. 1801
(SEVENTH EARL OF SHAFTESBURY)
COMMEMORATED IN THE ANGLICAN CHURCH ON 1 OCTOBER

If you had been living in Victorian days about 150 years ago, chances are that you would have been a full-time worker by the time you were 9 years old. You may have been down the coal mines, inside chimneys, or in the factory mills, crawling between machines to find loose threads. Life would have been pretty miserable. Anthony Ashley Cooper saw how bad it was for children and determined to do something about it.

Anthony Ashley was born in 1801. His wealthy family sent him to the 'public' school at Harrow, and then on to Christ Church College, Oxford. In 1826, as Lord Ashley, he became a Member of Parliament, and from the beginning of a long career in government he spoke up to defend the rights of children and of the poor. He believed that everyone should live in decent houses and that every child should have the opportunity to go to school. Lord Ashley was simply following his deep religious belief that every human being is equally important. He was an Evangelical Anglican who based his life on following the Gospel as best he could. He had seen how Jesus cared for the sick, for the poor and for children. That was his model.

Lord Ashley used his important position to put into practice his deep faith. And he succeeded. He led campaigns that eventually made it illegal for children under 13 years old to work in the factories or in the mines. He helped create schools for the poor, and better housing in the industrial towns. He even helped Florence Nightingale in her campaign to improve conditions for soldiers. Outside Parliament he supported the work of Anglican missionaries.

In 1851 Lord Ashley succeeded his father as the Seventh Earl of Shaftesbury, and so moved from Parliament to the House of Lords, where he continued to influence the Government on behalf of the poor. After his death in 1885 he was not forgotten. A street in central London is named after him, Shaftesbury Avenue. It leads to the famous Piccadilly Circus. In the centre of Piccadilly is the statue of Eros, put there as a memorial to Lord Ashley, Earl of Shaftesbury. Eros is the god of love. He holds an arrow, or 'shaft', in his hands. Christians remember that this noble politician was not inspired by a Greek god, but by the life of Jesus who showed him the human face of the loving God.

THINK ABOUT IT
Children under 10 still work in factories abroad making your clothes or your footballs. Is this fair?

BARTOLOMÉ DE LAS CASAS (CATHOLIC PRIEST) SIXTEENTH CENTURY

Have you ever been out with your family to watch a procession go up the High Street? It may be the Lord Mayor's parade, the local carnival, or even the return of the triumphant FA cup winners. A young boy called Bartolomé once stood on a street in Spain to cheer and welcome Christopher Columbus home from his first long sea voyage. Not long afterwards Bartolomé sailed with his father on Christopher Columbus' third voyage to the New World (Central and South America). Bartolomé had been born in Spain in the fifteenth century, and grew up in Seville. He was ordained in Hispaniola. He went to America with the *conquistadores*, the adventurers and soldiers who crossed the world in search of gold and other wealth.

The Spanish were Catholics and always took priests with them on their ships. Fra Bartolomé proved to be a handful. He soon grew distressed at what he saw. The soldiers were ruthless in forcing the local inhabitants (we call them indigenous Americans) to hand over their gold and their land. He wrote about it in an *Account of the Destruction of the Indies* in 1542. The book was banned by the church authorities. This was not because it was untrue, but because he wrote 'cruel and fierce things about Spanish soldiers'. Fra Bartolomé was horrified at the way the local people were treated and hated the way the landowners from Europe were using them.

He wrote: 'I have seen with my own eyes these gentle, peaceful people subjected to the most inhuman cruelties that have ever been committed by generations of cruel men. And this is for no other reason than insatiable greed, the hunger and thirst for gold on the part of our own people.'

Today some Spanish Dominican priests in Seville are asking the Pope to proclaim Fra Bartolomé as a saint. They believe that he had outstanding courage and a true understanding of the Gospel when he spoke out for the Native Americans. After all, Jesus himself spoke out on behalf of the poor and the outsiders. They regard Fra Bartolomé as the first human-rights campaigner. Today there are many people who suffer injustice by being pushed aside by the rich and power-ful. The priests believe that Fra Bartolomé is a shining example for anyone distressed by these injustices. They hope that more people could be inspired to speak out for the weak and those who are dispossessed of their land.

THINK ABOUT IT
Do you have the courage to speak out on behalf of others?

BARTOLOMÉ DE LAS CASAS
16th. CENTURY

Bernard of Aosta (sidebar)

BERNARD OF AOSTA
(PATRON SAINT OF TRAVELLERS)

D. 1081

FEAST DAY: 28 MAY

Do you have a dog? There is a strong breed of dog called the St Bernard. These sturdy brown and white dogs are able to adapt to freezing conditions in mountain snow. They became famous as mountain rescue dogs. These fine animals are named after St Bernard of Aosta.

There is not very much known about this St Bernard. The stories told about him may well be legends. These are stories that grow up around important people, but cannot be proved to have happened. Bernard certainly lived in the eleventh century at Annecy in France. He may have been the son of the Count of Menthon, since he is sometimes described as Bernard of Menthon. It was said that his parents arranged a suitable marriage for him, but he had set his heart on becoming a priest. On the eve of the wedding he disappeared and his family spent years searching for him far and wide.

Meanwhile Bernard had gone to the Bishop of Aosta in Italy, where he lived in hiding in the archdeacon's house. He was ordained a priest and later became an archdeacon himself. The diocese spread across the mountains among people living in small Alpine villages. Bernard spent 40 years visiting his people, walking or riding to remote hamlets in the mountains. The passes were snow-blocked in the winter and sometimes there were avalanches. Many travellers were lost. So Bernard built two travel lodges at the summits of the high Alpine passes, later called after him – the Little and Great St Bernard Passes. Travellers could take shelter from storms and refresh themselves.

The legend says that Bernard's parents, still searching for their long-lost son, rested in one of the lodges. And there he was. What a reunion! He invited a group of Augustinian Canons to look after the pilgrims and travellers crossing the mountains to and from Italy. It was this order of priests who first used strong dogs as mountain rescuers in the seventeenth century. The breed is perfect for that task. They are sure-footed on ice and snow, and have a sense of smell that helps them to find people buried under the snow. Over the years the dogs saved thousands of lives. The priests still run the lodges today, but they only keep St Bernard dogs as pets. Modern rescue services have replaced the animals.

St Bernard dogs are known for their loyalty, gentleness and patience, virtues that the saint was said to possess. That is why the dogs are so well named.

THINK ABOUT IT
What is your outstanding virtue?

BERNARD OF AOSTA
DIED 1081

Camillus de Lellis

CAMILLUS DE LELLIS (PATRON SAINT OF NURSES)

D. 1614

FEAST DAY: 14 JULY

What do you know about giants? I'll describe one to you: An enormous figure more than six foot six inches tall with very broad shoulders; fierce, bad-tempered, violent and very frightening when he stares at you with his piercing black eyes. This is not a giant in a story book, but a man called Camillus who was born in the Abruzzi region of Italy in the year 1550. His story is more interesting than the traditional fairy tale of giants and ogres.

Camillus was only 17 years old when he joined his elderly soldier father in the Venetian army. They went to war against Turkish invaders, and Camillus received a serious leg wound which affected him for the rest of his life. His father died after that war and Camillus became a rebellious young man. He gambled heavily, got into fights and was the despair of his family. He was the local thug. By the age of 24 he was utterly destitute. It was then that a remarkable thing happened. Our awful ogre became a gentle giant.

Some Capuchin (hooded) Franciscan friars took pity on the desolate Camillus. After listening to one of the friars preaching at Mass, he was a changed man. We call this a conversion, a turn-around. He asked to join the Capuchin friars but was refused because of his bad leg. Instead he went to a hospital for the incurably sick in Rome, and devoted the rest of his life to nursing the poor. The conditions at the hospital were unimaginable. Camillus was shocked to find patients left to rot in filth, and even taken to the mortuary before they were dead.

Other young men joined Camillus, determined to serve the sick with compassion. With the support of St Philip Neri, Camillus became a priest and founded the 'Servants of the Poor', a congregation of male nurses. They promised to look after the sick at home and in hospital, as well as victims of the plague and prisoners. The members are now known as Camillans, and the gentle giant is sometimes called the Red Cross saint, because his congregation wear a black habit with a red cross on the chest. Camillus founded eight hospitals in Italy where he introduced 'new' ideas for the care of the sick. He insisted on fresh air, proper diets and isolation wards for infected patients. He sent nurses to battlefields with the first recorded military ambulance units.

Camillus was in pain from his diseased leg most of his life. Perhaps this is why he had such compassion for the sick, spending every day at their bedside for nearly 40 years. He had taken to heart the words of Jesus: 'When I was sick you visited me.'

THINK ABOUT IT
Be very grateful for our nurses and doctors.

CAMILLUS DE LELLIS DIED 1614

CAROLINE CHISHOLM (WIFE AND MOTHER)

D. 1877

A ROMAN CATHOLIC COMMEMORATED BY THE ANGLICAN CHURCH ON 16 MAY

Caroline Chisholm

In the middle of the nineteenth century, the most famous woman in England apart from Queen Victoria was Caroline Chisholm. Born near Northampton in 1808, she was baptised in the Church of England. Her mother encouraged her to help the poor, and her generous nature caught the attention of a Catholic man, Archibald Chisholm. They were married in 1830. She became a Catholic, and he promised to support her works of charity.

Archibald was an officer in the East India Company's army, and the young couple went out to Madras. In 1838 the family took holiday leave in Australia and their lives were transformed. They were appalled at the distress of the immigrants arriving in what was a 'convict' colony. Men had no work, women looking for work or for husbands had been badly treated by ships' officers, and on arrival many ended up destitute and on the streets. The English couple began a campaign to improve conditions and change emigration and immigration laws in Britain and Australia. Caroline's work was difficult, especially as her husband had to return to India to complete army service. She got no help from the Governor or local people. She met the women from the ships and found them homes. Eventually she was able to reopen the abandoned rat-infested hostel set up earlier by Elizabeth Fry. She moved in and renovated it for the women. Caroline's biggest obstacle was the prejudice generally felt against Roman Catholics. But her eloquence and goodness won the day, especially when the Anglican bishop told his clergy to help her.

After seven years, and with no official authority, Caroline managed to settle over 11,000 people and reunite 600 families. She set up agencies in Australia to look after the interests of the immigrants. In 1846 she and her husband returned to London, and persuaded the Government, the House of Lords, the Colonial Office and Emigration Authority to improve every aspect of emigration. She was supported by Lord Shaftesbury, whilst she and Charles Dickens wrote letters, pamphlets and stories to the press. She set up groups to help emigrants prepare for leaving the country, and her husband returned to Australia to continue work there. Some years later Caroline and their six children were reunited with him in Australia.

Remarkably this busy lady never neglected her own children. She invented stories for them, and let them run around her desk and also accompany her on errands. The family ended up poor (they sold a gold medal presented by the Pope!) because they kept giving everything away; but they were always happy. It is no wonder that Australia remembers Caroline with affection and admiration. She has appeared on banknotes and stamps, and has been called 'The greatest woman pioneer in Australia'. She only achieved this because of her great religious faith and compassion.

THINK ABOUT IT
Caroline respected immigrants. Do you?

CAROLINE CHISHOLM
DIED 1877

Catherine of Alexandria

CATHERINE OF ALEXANDRIA (SAINT AND MARTYR) FOURTH CENTURY
FEAST DAY: 25 NOVEMBER

What sort of fireworks do you have on 5 November? Squibs, rockets, Roman candles? You may have Catherine wheels, those circular coiled firecrackers that are pinned to the wall, and whizz around spurting out fiery sparks. The firework is named after the fourth-century martyr, Catherine of Alexandria.

Devotion to St Catherine grew in the ninth century when a monastery named after her was built at the foot of Mount Sinai. She later became one of the most popular saints in the Middle Ages, and can be seen in stained glass windows in ancient churches. But not very much is really known about her, and her story reads like legend. She is said to have been born into a noble family in Alexandria, and since she was learned and beautiful the Emperor Maxentius wanted to marry her. But she refused.

The emperor was rather in awe of Catherine because of her outspoken courage. She boldly complained to him that people were forced to worship idols (false gods). Maxentius called in 50 philosophers – very learned 'thinkers' – to argue with her and show her that the Christian faith was wrong. But to everyone's amazement she won all the arguments. The emperor sent the 50 men to their deaths because of their failure. That is when he asked Catherine to marry him. She told him that it was not possible, because she was 'wedded to Christ'. He was furious, and had her beaten for two hours before throwing her into prison.

The story goes that even in her cell Catherine was calm. A dove came to feed her and Christ appeared to her in a vision. The emperor's wife visited her and was so impressed that she became a Christian. Maxentius was angry. He had Catherine tied to a rotating wheel. But when it turned it broke into splinters. Pieces flew into the crowd, killing some of the bystanders. It is this image that is the basis for our fireworks. Eventually the young saint was executed by the sword.

Many women martyrs are honoured by the Church. But Catherine is unusual. It is surprising that in the fourth century a woman is represented as arguing philosophy with learned men. She has naturally been chosen as patron saint of craftsmen and women who work with wheels – potters, weavers, and cycle or car mechanics – as well as of students and philosophers. Every year on St Catherine's feast day, at some of the training colleges for priests, the philosophers have to entertain the other students. She is highly regarded.

THINK ABOUT IT
Do you have enough courage to speak up for what you believe in?

CATHERINE OF ALEXANDRIA 4TH CENTURY

CHICO MENDES (CATHOLIC WORKER)

D. 1988

KILLED FOR STANDING UP FOR WORKERS' RIGHTS AND THE ENVIRONMENT

Chico Mendes

Do you collect money in your school for CAFOD, Christian Aid or Tear Fund? These are three Christian organisations which aid progress and development in parts of the world hit by poverty and inequality. Their task is also to educate the wealthy nations about the needs of the underprivileged.

CAFOD is the Catholic organisation that campaigns for justice in this way. Some years ago it brought to our attention the plight of the workers at rubber estates in Brazil. In 1988 one of the workers was shot because he led a union movement to improve conditions and prevent the forests from being destroyed. CAFOD told his story. He was called Chico Mendes.

Francisco 'Chico' Alves Mendes was born on the Cachoeira rubber estate in north-west Brazil. He was unable to go to school like you; it was forbidden by the landowners. They kept their workers illiterate so that they could cheat them in their wages. Chico was a full-time worker as a rubber tapper by the time he was 9 years old. In the 1960s cattle ranchers from the south needed more pasture. Beefburgers had become very popular, and South American farmers were offered good money to graze the cattle.

The rubber estate collapsed as the trees were felled for pasture. Tappers like Chico lost everything. One day a stranger passed Chico's house and stopped to talk with him. It changed his life. Tavora was an educated man who had come to live in the area to try and save some of the rubber estates. Over the next few years he taught Chico to read, and introduced him to the trade union. This is an organisation that tries to protect the rights of people at their work. In 1968, when Chico Mendes was only 23 years old, he was ready to organise a union of the rubber tappers in his home town of Xapuri. But it met with much opposition and died out. A few years later he and his friends joined a trade union in Brasilia. They were encouraged by their church leaders who had set up training days.

Full of confidence, Chico returned home to help the local struggling families by telling them their rights. He set up peaceful protests against the destruction of the environment, and the loss of jobs. His family and the whole community were shocked when Chico was betrayed by the parish priest of Xapuri, who was a friend of the rich landowners. The landowners sought out the 'trouble-maker' and killed him. Chico's wife and children continue his work today, helped by the Catholic Church.

THINK ABOUT IT
What can you do to protect the environment?

CLARE OF ASSISI (SAINT)   D. 1253

FEAST DAY: 11 AUGUST

St Clare of Assisi is the patron saint of television. This is very strange because she lived in the thirteenth century, seven centuries before television was invented. So who was she? Clare came from a noble family in Assisi, Italy. When she was 11 years old, and being introduced into the elegant society of her town, Assisi was shaken by the actions of a local young man called Francis. His father was a rich merchant, so he could have expected a large inheritance and a comfortable life. But he turned his back on it and began roaming the countryside, begging from the rich and giving to the poor. All of Assisi was astonished. He was the talk of the town.

Young Clare listened to the talk about Francis, and was captivated and inspired by his example. Other young men of the neighbourhood were impressed by his joyful simplicity and generosity. They recognised that the freedom Francis had found in the way he lived the Gospel brought great joy to everyone. Many joined him, and soon the little band of friends was accepted and the gossip stopped.

But Clare did not stop thinking about Francis and his way of following Jesus. By the time she was 18 years old she had turned down two offers of marriage, and set her heart on following Francis' way of life. She left home one night and turned up at his friary (religious house). Seeing how determined she was, he cut her hair off and gave her a simple dress of rough cloth to replace her fine clothes. He asked some Benedictine nuns to take her in. Her family were distraught.

Under Francis' guidance Clare prepared to live a life of great poverty. When other young women joined her, Francis gave them the house next door to the Church of San Damiano in Assisi. He wrote a 'rule of life' for them, and this was the beginning of a religious order called the 'Poor Ladies'. Today they are known as the 'Poor Clares'. Clare became the first abbess, and remained in this post until she died 40 years later. She never went outside the convent again. Later her sister Agnes joined her, and then her widowed mother too. The little community became a shining example of compassion and goodness to their neighbours. They lived in great poverty themselves, yet gave to those in need around them.

Clare was loved and admired for her joyful courage and holiness. She suffered bad health yet never complained. At the end of her life Clare was too ill to attend Mass. It is said that she could see an image of the service on the wall of her cell – the first 'miraculous' television. This is why she is named its patron.

THINK ABOUT IT
Riches don't always bring happiness but sometimes poverty does.

DIED 1253

CLARE OF ASSISI

THE DALAI LAMA (BUDDHIST)

B. 1935

A SAINTLY MAN

There is a saying, 'Smile and the whole world smiles with you.' A man called the Dalai Lama is known to have a wonderful smile. Someone wrote: 'He has the most beautiful smile, which will appear at the most unexpected moments . . . It is one of those smiles that is like the sun breaking through, and you never forget it.' The Dalai Lama has been called the 'Laughing Buddha'. Why is this? And who is he?

His family name is Tenzin Gyatso, and he is the Buddhist leader of the people of Tibet. He is the fourteenth leader, or Dalai Lama. Today he is recognised as one of the most respected and admired world leaders of peace. His wonderful smile hides great pain and heartache, because he is at present living in exile in India. He is joined by 100,000 other Tibetans.

Tibet is a large country next to China. When Tenzin was only 15 years old and already the chosen religious leader of Tibet, China invaded the country. That was over 50 years ago. Ever since, the Chinese Government has tried to crush the rich, ancient culture of Tibet, especially its Buddhist faith.

Buddhism differs from other religions because it does not speak of God. Lord Buddha was born 500 years before Jesus. He was puzzled by the suffering he saw around him: poverty, old age, disease and death. He thought about it and began to teach that by accepting suffering we can escape from it. He said that if we stopped saying, 'I want . . ., me . . ., mine . . .', we would be able to reach the peaceful state called 'Nirvana'. Buddhism spread across most of India, south-east Asia, and the Far East. Some Indian teachers took it to Tibet. Tibetan Buddhists are known for their teaching about compassion. Their teaching is like Jesus' teaching – that we must treat everyone, even our enemies, with goodness and understanding. The Dalai Lama said: 'One of the most important things is compassion. You cannot buy it in one of New York's big shops. You cannot produce it by machine. You must develop it inside yourself.'

The Dalai Lama's people suffer badly under Chinese rule, but he insists that they 'fight' the injustice in the Buddhist non-violent way. He teaches about peace to the whole world. And always with his big smile.

THINK ABOUT IT
Smile and the whole world smiles with you.

DALAI LAMA
BORN 1935

Desmond Tutu

DESMOND TUTU (ANGLICAN)   B. 1931
RETIRED ARCHBISHOP OF CAPE TOWN

Have you heard of the Nobel Peace Prize? It is awarded annually to the person considered to have worked hardest to bring about peace in the world. One winner was a South African churchman called Desmond Tutu. Alongside a remarkable leader, Nelson Mandela, he became the symbol of hope and justice for black people in South Africa.

Desmond was born in Klerksdorp in 1931. His family were poor, even though his father was the headteacher of the Methodist school. One day Desmond and his mother were astonished when a white priest greeted them in the street. White people did not talk to his people. The white Government had a system called 'Apartheid' which kept the races apart. The priest was an English Anglican missionary called Trevor Huddleston. He became friends with the Tutu family and visited Desmond when he was very ill.

The schools for black children had few facilities, but Desmond was a good student and worked hard. He wanted to be a doctor but could not pay the fees. Instead he became a teacher and later married Leah. They had four children. He taught at the high school next door to his father's primary school. But this was the 1950s, when the Apartheid system was causing terrible hardship to his people. The black, white, Indian and coloured communities were ordered to live and work separately. Only the white population had the right to vote. They had all the privileges.

Schooling for black children became impossible under this racist Government. Desmond knew something had to be done. With the help of Fr Huddleston he trained for the priesthood in England. When he returned to South Africa he became a strong and outspoken opponent of the Government. When he became Dean of Johannesburg, the family could have lived in the official house as 'honorary whites'. They chose to live in Soweto, the poor black township. Desmond believed that his priestly role was to live and suffer hardship with his people. He spoke out and led them in peaceful demonstrations.

No one was surprised when this smiling, bubbly priest eventually became the Archbishop of Cape Town, the leader of the Anglican Church in South Africa. He continued to challenge the politicians over their ruthless and unjust laws. Eventually success came, and in 1994 black South Africans were able to vote for the first time. They chose Nelson Mandela as their leader. The new black Government set up a remarkable inquiry into the years of injustice and abuse of human rights. Instead of sending the guilty white politicians to prison, the 'Truth and Reconciliation Commission' asked them to explain and confess their wrongdoing in public. By doing this they would be forgiven and reconciled to those they had oppressed. It was a system based on a Christian understanding of forgiveness. It was appropriate that Desmond Tutu led the proceedings.

THINK ABOUT IT
Could you forgive someone who treated you badly?

DESMOND TUTU
B▫ 1931▫

DUNSTAN (SAINT)
FEAST DAY: 19 MAY

D. 988

Dunstan

Dunstan is not very well known as a saint. But he should be, because he is patron saint of goldsmiths, jewellers, locksmiths, armourers, blacksmiths, musicians and singers. You can probably tell from this that he was an artistic craftsman. But he was much more than this, and in the tenth century he was one of the leading figures in England. It is said that he shaped the history of England for the future.

Dunstan was born into a noble Anglo-Saxon family in 910, in the kingdom of the west Saxons (Wessex). It was a time when young people were often given high office. Edgar became King of Wessex at the age of 16, and Dunstan was elected Abbot of Glastonbury when he was only 18 years old. Being the artist and scholar he was, he soon turned Glastonbury into a centre of civilisation. He painted and illuminated manuscripts, and designed beautiful patterns for church embroidery. He learnt to craft metal so that he could make church bells and the sacred cups and patens for Mass. He was also a great musician, singing and playing the harp. His many talents inspired others to share his creative spirit, and Glastonbury became famous for the arts.

Dunstan needed to design and make new equipment for his church because the monasteries and churches had been stripped in the Danish raids. Everything of value had been looted. Once he had put his own church in order, the young abbot set about restoring monastic life to the whole of the country. The leading noble families, who recognised his talents and intelligence, asked his advice. He told them to make peace with the Danes. They were not very happy about this, and even less happy when he told them off for their bad behaviour. He was sent into exile in Flanders. That was where he discovered the Benedictine monasteries. They were exactly what he wanted to introduce back into England.

The new king, the 16-year-old Edgar, called him back home to become his royal adviser, and appointed him as Bishop of Worcester. He later became Bishop of London and finally, in 961, Archbishop of Canterbury. As head of the Church in England he was able to renew and reform the monasteries across the whole land. He held a conference with all the bishops, abbots and abbesses. They agreed to return to the sensible Rule of St Benedict.

The most important change that Dunstan brought about was to encourage the monks to share their lives with the local people. He said that monks and nuns must serve the community. The monks were the educated people, and they should share their knowledge of medicine and agriculture with their neighbours. They opened the first schools. They built guest houses where people could stay for a quiet and prayerful rest. They continue this hospitality today.

THINK ABOUT IT
Do you have an artistic skill you can share with others?

DUNSTAN DIED '88

Eglantyne Jebb

EGLANTYNE JEBB (SOCIAL REFORMER)

D. 1928

COMMEMORATED IN THE ANGLICAN CHURCH ON 17 DECEMBER

Eglantyne Jebb is a rather unusual name. But then Eglantyne was a rather unusual lady. She was born into an extraordinary Victorian family, in 1876. Her father was a well-educated landowner, and a fervent Christian. Mr Jebb invited the servants and farm workers and all their children to meet regularly to discuss important issues. He listened to everyone's opinion. Meanwhile his wife did all she could to make the servants' and workers' lives more interesting. She gave them lessons in wood-carving, painting, basket-making and carpentry. It was a very happy household

Eglantyne joyfully applied for a place at Oxford University. She was one of the first women to go there. And she loved it. She studied hard but found time for dancing and sport. She liked rowing and was a good hockey player. She became a teacher. When she visited her pupils' homes, she was horrified by the poverty, and understood why some of them were difficult to teach. Eglantyne was happiest when she could escape to the hillsides and spend time in prayer. She said that time spent alone, 'finding delight in the beauty of nature, literature and art, was a heaven on earth'.

Then Eglantyne had an experience which she said shaped the rest of her life. There was a cheap print of Christ crowned with thorns hanging on the wall. She looked at the suffering in Christ's eyes. She immediately knew that all her sufferings (and she had poor health) were swallowed up in his pain. From that moment Eglantyne looked for the best way to serve Christ in others, at whatever cost to herself. She chose to help children who were in greatest need.

In 1912, when war broke out in the Balkans, Eglantyne joined some of her family in northern Greece to help the thousands of refugees. Seeing children dying of sickness and starvation, she returned to England to raise money to save their lives. With her sister Dorothy, Eglantyne founded the 'Save the Children Fund'. It was not easy; she was prosecuted for handing out leaflets showing starving babies. Many people did help her, especially Pope Benedict XV, who asked the Catholic Church to support the work. This led to approval from the Anglican, Orthodox and Free Churches. Her Children's Fund fed and housed refugee children, and built schools and homes for children with disabilities.

Eglantyne worked for the poor in Russia, the Balkans, Africa, India and China, and her lasting work was to draw up a 'Children's Charter' of human rights. In 1924 it was accepted by the League of Nations. When she died, aged 52, she was called a 'saint' by all who knew her. They said she was beautiful to look at, but even more beautiful within.

THINK ABOUT IT
Raise some money to support Save the Children Fund.

EGLANTINE JEBB
DIED 1928

ELIAS CHACOUR (CATHOLIC PRIEST)

B. 1938

WORKER FOR RECONCILIATION

Elias was born in the village of Biram in Galilee, amongst the same hills where Jesus probably played as a boy. Elias was one of six children, and his Palestinian parents were very proud of living near Nazareth. The family could trace their Christian heritage back to the first century. They lived simply and peacefully alongside their Jewish neighbours. Elias learnt from his parents to love and respect everyone, whatever their race or religion. His father was content to work in the fields amongst his olive trees. His mother could not read or write, but she knew the Gospel by heart. Elias loved to listen to her telling him stories about Jesus, their own 'Man of Galilee'.

One day in 1947, when the Second World War was over, Mr Chacour was excited. News had come that some Jews would return to Palestine. He told the family that they must welcome them home as their brothers and sisters. They all belonged to Galilee. Unfortunately these returning Jews (called Zionists) had ferocious political plans. They destroyed the Palestinian homes and took away the men, including Elias' father and elder brother. Thousands of Palestinians were killed and many forced into refugee camps. The Chacour family were eventually reunited, but never returned to their beloved home in Biram.

Elias was bewildered, frightened and sad. But his parents continued to remind the children that Jesus had told them to love the people who hurt you, and to try and make peace. Elias knew that his mother's favourite story was Jesus preaching 'Blessed are the peacemakers'. He decided he must spend the rest of his life working to help Palestinian Christians and Muslims to live peacefully alongside the Jewish people. He went away to school, and then in 1954 he became a student at the Catholic Melchite Seminary in Nazareth. He had to go to Paris to become a qualified teacher, but later was the first Palestinian to earn a degree from the Hebrew (Jewish) University in Jerusalem.

When he was ordained a priest, Elias was sent to a small village called Ibillin, to rebuild the broken-down church. He quietly set about repairing it and inviting the local Galilean community to come together. He started a remarkable project. With little help from his superiors he built a school, and invited Catholic, Jewish and Muslim students to attend. Fr Chacour is still the priest of Ibillin, and today thousands of students are educated in his school and college. He is a busy man, speaks 11 languages, and has built libraries and community centres across Galilee. He is mainly funded by American Evangelical Christians, because the traditional churches are not too enthusiastic that he teaches Muslims and Jews.

But to many ordinary Christians, Fr Chacour is a living reminder of the Man of Galilee who walked the same hills, and opened his heart to love everyone.

THINK ABOUT IT
When you are tempted to have an argument, stop and keep the peace.

ELIAS
CHACOUR
B = 1938

Elizabeth Fry

ELIZABETH FRY
(QUAKER AND PRISON REFORMER)
D. 1845
REMEMBERED ON 12 OCTOBER

Can you imagine what it would be like to have 10 brothers and sisters? One thing is certain. You would have a very tired mother. Many people know that Elizabeth Fry is famous for visiting and helping the women in Newgate prison. They don't all know that she was the mother of 11 children. Elizabeth admitted that she sometimes got things wrong, and neglected her family for her prisoners. But after her death two of her daughters described her as a saint.

Elizabeth was born at Earlham in Norfolk in 1780 into the Gurney family, who were wealthy Quaker bankers who lived a comfortable life. She married Joseph Fry, a London merchant and a strict Quaker. As a serious and religious woman, Elizabeth grew impatient with the household duties of a businessman's wife. She hated entertaining guests and overseeing the servants' duties. Then in 1810 she was elected as a preacher. This gave her the freedom to leave her family home on missions of charity.

Elizabeth became an energetic preacher, travelling up and down the country. After a few years the terrible state of Newgate prison came to her attention. She was shaken by the condition of the women and children there; she described them as 'wild beasts'. This was the turning point in her life. After facing much opposition, especially from the authorities, she succeeded in starting a school inside the prison for the children, and organising sewing classes for their mothers. She insisted that the prisons should be run with dignity and that the prisoners should be treated with respect. She hated the death penalty, and sat comforting the condemned women before they were executed.

At first the Government listened to this strong woman: she was known to make important officials get on their knees to pray with her! She took on other campaigns – a night shelter for the homeless in London, better facilities on the ships taking convicts to Australia, and proper care for the mentally ill. She set up the first training centre for nurses in Kaiserswerth, Germany. One of their students was Florence Nightingale. At the same time she supported the training of Protestant Sisters of Charity at Guy's Hospital. They became known as the 'Fry Sisters', and several of them went with Florence Nightingale to Scutari. In the last years of her life she made many visits abroad, to explain her work to European kings and government ministers.

Elizabeth had a hard life. She was accused of neglecting her children, her husband became bankrupt, and the Government finally refused to accept her prison reforms. It was said that she had no sense of humour. Yet all agreed that her love for the poor and the outcast was so overwhelming that somehow it made her attractive. She is an example of a saintly person who made the comfortable feel uncomfortable.

THINK ABOUT IT
Saints can be very hard to live with. Why?

ELIZABETH
FRY
B · 1780 · D · 1845 ·

ELIZABETH SETON (SAINT)   D. 1821
FEAST DAY: 4 JANUARY

Elizabeth Seton

Catholic children in New York will know all about Elizabeth Ann Seton. She is the first native-born American citizen to be officially recognised as a saint by the Catholic Church. Elizabeth was born in 1774 and was from a Protestant family. She married William Magee Seton, a wealthy New York businessman. He was a good and loving husband.

Their marriage was a very happy one, but it ended tragically when William died of tuberculosis after only nine years. During that time they had had five children – three girls and two boys. The family were on holiday in Italy when William was taken ill and died. Elizabeth and the children stayed on for another six months, living with a sympathetic Italian family. Their kindness impressed Elizabeth and probably influenced her decision to become a Catholic. In 1805, two years later, she was received into the Catholic Church in New York.

The next few years for Elizabeth were difficult and lonely. Some of her family and friends avoided her, because they disagreed with her decision. She missed her husband dreadfully, and had a great struggle to support her young family. Eventually a priest invited them all to Baltimore, where Elizabeth could earn a living by opening a school for girls. Other women soon joined her, and in 1809 they moved into a larger house in Maryland. They had formed a small community, which was soon to be recognised as a new religious congregation.

Elizabeth was practical and prayerful. She was the natural leader of the community, and was known as Mother Seton. They took the name 'Sisters of Charity'. Elizabeth did not abandon her own children. They lived with her, and she cared for them even when they were away at school, and later when they started work.

Mother Seton is dearly loved in America, because she began what is known as the parochial school system, which is still at the centre of parish life right across the United States. During her lifetime her community were invited to start up these schools along the East Coast. They built orphanages too, and took care of anyone in need in the neighbourhood. Elizabeth Seton died in 1821. She was only 47 years old, a young mother of five children who had become a mother to many more. All her life she had been aware that Jesus said: 'If any-one gives you a cup of water as a friend of mine, they're doing God's work.'

THINK ABOUT IT
How often do you do God's work?

ELIZABETH SETON
DIED 1821

Francis de Sales

FRANCIS DE SALES (SAINT) D. 1622
FEAST DAY: 24 JANUARY

St Francis de Sales is the patron saint of the author of this book, because he is patron of writers and journalists. Although he lived about 400 years ago, some of his writings are still read with appreciation today. Francis was born into an aristocratic family in the Château de Sales in Savoy (France). He studied law in Paris and Padua, because he was expected to take a responsible position in the Government of Savoy. But Francis had other ideas, and his father was not happy.

With gentle but firm words, Francis persuaded his family that he should become a priest. He was to become one of the most important figures in the Catholic Church in the seventeenth century; and a much-loved bishop. On becoming a priest his first task was difficult, even dangerous. He was sent to preach to the followers of John Calvin, who was one of the sixteenth-century 'protesters' against the power and corrupt practices of the Catholic Church. Many Catholics in Geneva had become Calvinists, and Francis was given the job of persuading them to return to the Church of Rome. He and his companions were often insulted, beaten up and their lives threatened.

But eventually Francis was successful, and by the end of his mission it was believed that around 8,000 people returned to their original faith. A Calvinist minister in Geneva even wrote: 'If we honoured any man as a saint, I know no one since the days of the apostles more worthy of it than this man Francis.' How did this happen? He was respected by everyone simply because he respected them. He became known for his polite, good manners and gentleness. When he became Bishop of Geneva in 1602, Francis said that he would be bishop only in public, but remain ordinary Francis de Sales in private. He never wanted power or special treatment.

Geneva was a very difficult diocese. The new bishop set about reforming and reorganising it; he wanted his people to follow the Gospel with a new simplicity. For centuries, religious writings had been read by monks and nuns only. Lay people seemed to be excluded. Francis changed this. He began writing leaflets addressed to ordinary people. Like a good psychologist, he understood people and knew exactly how to help them. He said it was not difficult for 'soldiers, shopkeepers and office workers, royalty and married couples' to live holy lives. In his pamphlets and private letters to individuals he encouraged everyone to think often during each day of the love of God. He said that we can pray anywhere: in the street, at work or study, and in the midst of family tasks.

St Francis de Sales wrote two best-selling books. In them he wrote about God's great love for everyone. He kept repeating that God is to be found in our ordinary lives. They were the favourite books of King James I and John Wesley, and they are still read today.

THINK ABOUT IT
Say a quiet prayer on the way to school.

FRANCIS DE SALES
DIED 1622

FRANCIS XAVIER (MISSIONARY AND SAINT)

D. 1552

FEAST DAY: 3 DECEMBER

Francis Xavier

Do you know anyone who is so energetic and enthusiastic that you cannot keep up with them? Francis Xavier was one of those people. He could quite wear you out. Francis was born in 1506 in the Basque region of Spain. He was of noble family and studied in Paris, where he met Ignatius of Loyola. The meeting changed his life. He and five companions joined Ignatius, and the small group dedicated their lives to God. This was the beginning of the Jesuit Order of priests.

In the sixteenth century the Catholic Church firmly believed that unbaptised people would not go to heaven. This thought horrified Francis, so he volunteered to go to unknown parts of the world to convert 'pagans' to the Christian faith. Explorers and missionaries had gone west to the Americas, but the East was still something of a mystery. So in 1541, with two others, he set out on a voyage of discovery to spread the faith.

It took 13 months to reach Goa on the coast of India. It became their headquarters for the next seven years, during which time Francis set up Christian communities in southern India, Ceylon (Sri Lanka), the Molucca Islands of the East Indies, and on the Malay Peninsula. Wherever Francis stayed, he lived as the poor did, only eating rice and drinking water, and sleeping on the ground in discomfort. No hardship was too much for such an enthusiastic preacher.

Francis was travelling with the authority of the Catholic Church, but also as the representative of the King of Portugal. In 1549 he reached Japan, where he was received with courtesy and interest. This part of his mission was quite different. He was entertained by the rich merchants and noblemen, and given permission to preach by the authorities. He had learnt some Japanese and could communicate well with his audience. Francis changed his almost fanatical method of teaching about the Gospel. In India he had insisted that all 'pagan' attitudes be totally wiped out. But he was impressed by the honesty, love of learning, politeness and, above all, the sense of honour that he found in the Japanese. He changed his style, and began to teach about Christ by building on the virtues the people already had. After two years he was ready to move on.

Francis wanted to reach China, his final goal. He was trying to arrange to be smuggled into the mainland because China did not welcome foreigners. He reached the island of Shangchwan, near the mouth of the Canton River, where he waited for a Chinese junk to take him to the mainland secretly. There he caught a fever and died alone except for a young Chinese Christian who had come with him from Goa. He was only 46 years old. Francis was buried in Goa, which has kept the Catholic faith he planted there until today. His first style of converting people is not acceptable today, but his enthusiasm and willingness to suffer make him an appropriate patron saint of missionaries.

THINK ABOUT IT
Make sure you are enthusiastic about the right things.

GANDHI (HINDU LEADER)   D. 1948
ADMIRED AND RESPECTED BY PEOPLE OF ALL RELIGIONS

Gandhi

Mohandas Gandhi was born in 1869 in Porpandar, India. He was a very quiet, shy boy. His mother always left a light burning in his room at night because he was frightened of ghosts. He was even more terrified of snakes, and there were many snakes in India. He was still very young when his parents arranged his marriage with a young girl called Kasturbai. Mohandas decided to become a lawyer, and when he was 19 years old he came to London for his studies. At this time India was ruled by England.

Gandhi had always realised that there were bad things wrong with the world, especially the fact that some people were not free. He wanted his country to be free from the British. He was horrified when he took a job in South Africa to discover that his Indian people there were treated like slaves. He spent the rest of his life struggling peacefully for change. Gandhi hated violence and racial and religious prejudice. He firmly believed that all people were equal.

The shy schoolboy had become a very bold young man. He kept telling his Indian people that they must 'fight' the British Government for their human rights. But he told them to 'fight' with love and respect, never with violence. He hated war and destruction. Gandhi led his people in 'disobedient' campaigns where they marched in defiance of the law. He once led a 200-mile march to the sea to collect salt. It was a protest against the Government who had total control of it. Unfortunately some of his campaigns ended in violence, in spite of his insistence on peace. Sometimes he was arrested, and at other times he was invited to work with the Government on reforms. He was delighted when, in 1947, Britain gave India its independence.

Gandhi was a Hindu. The poorest Hindus were called 'untouchables' and given all the dirty jobs. They were never allowed to earn much money. Gandhi would not accept that these poor families were less important than the rich ones. He called these 'untouchables' the 'children of God'. He was not very popular amongst his own people for saying this. He sometimes fasted from food to make people sit up and listen. His teaching and example are very important for the whole world. He once said, 'Hindus, Muslims, Christians – all should love each other and respect what the other person believes.' If people did this there would be no wars.

The quiet boy became famous as a peace-loving man, who showed everyone that peaceful actions can change the world. He once questioned the Jewish law which permitted revenge, by saying, 'If you take an eye for an eye, soon everyone will be blind.' Sadly Gandhi was killed by a Hindu who didn't like to be told to live at peace with Muslim neighbours. Like Jesus, this good man died because he believed that we are all God's children.

THINK ABOUT IT
Are you brave enough to walk away from a fight?

GANDHI
DIED • 1948

HENRIETTA BARNETT D. 1936
(CHRISTIAN SOCIAL REFORMER)
COMMEMORATED, WITH HER HUSBAND, BY THE ANGLICAN CHURCH ON 17 JUNE

Henrietta Barnett

It would be wrong to write about Henrietta Barnett without mentioning her husband, the Reverend Samuel Barnett. They worked together as a strong team to make life better for the poor in Victorian London. When Samuel became the vicar of St Jude's Church in Whitechapel, he became interested in the work of a lady called Octavia Hill, who was organising better housing for the poor. One of Octavia's assistants was Henrietta Rowland, a Londoner born in 1851. Henrietta and Samuel married when she was 22 years old, and for over 40 years they shared a great enthusiasm for helping others.

Samuel was not like many other nineteenth-century priests, who often blamed the poor for their poverty and preached stern words about avoiding sin and the devil. Samuel used a different method, which was sometimes criticised. He and Henrietta worked out ways of encouraging people to improve their lives. They didn't blame people for getting into fights or stealing money; they blamed the poverty that made them desperate. In those days there was no public money for making life easier for the community. It was usually people like the Barnetts who found ways to improve things.

Together with others, Samuel and Henrietta set up the Charity Organisation Society. Its main work was to find cheaper ways of housing the poor. Over the years, they were able to improve education and work opportunities for the Whitechapel families. The couple were heavily criticised for starting evening classes and entertainments in the parish. But they were deeply concerned at the great gap between the rich and the poor. Rich people had many opportunities for relaxation and pleasure. The poor had nothing. So Henrietta started discussion groups, and reading and art classes. Samuel even set up the Whitechapel Art Gallery for the students to display their work. He was always distressed that the poor never had the chance to go to university as he had done. He founded Toynbee Hall, where the working classes and those educated at university could meet.

Eventually, before his death in 1913, he was recognised by the Government, which appointed him as their Poor Law Guardian, and praised by the Church. Henrietta lived another 23 years, becoming the new Poor Law Guardian. She built schools for girls, and founded a charity to provide country holidays for slum children. She founded a new type of community in London, called Hampstead Garden Suburb. It was the first time that all classes of people were given the opportunity to live side by side.

Samuel and Henrietta could have lived selfish and comfortable lives, but they chose instead to work tirelessly for others. This was often at great cost to themselves.

THINK ABOUT IT
Families that support one another are happy families.

HENRIETTA
BARNETT
DIED 1936

HILDEGARD (SAINT)

FEAST DAY: 17 SEPTEMBER

D. 1179

Hildegard

Do you like poetry? If you look at a poetry book on the school or library shelf, you will probably find some good poems about the world of nature. There will be poems about water and rivers, and about fields and flowers. There will be others about the sky with its clouds, the sun, stars and moon. Go and have a look. A long time ago, over 900 years, a lady called Hildegard was writing poems, songs and music about the world of nature. She had grown up in the beautiful Rhine valley in Germany, and from a very early age she said that all the world around her was 'lit up by God'.

Hildegard had nine older brothers and sisters. When she was only 8 years old, her parents sent her away to boarding school. She was looked after by a remarkable lady called Jutta. It was Jutta who taught her about God and how to pray to him. Hildegard never forgot her teacher and all that she had learnt, even when she later became a nun. Hildegard wanted to spend all of her life thinking about God and his creation. And she did just that.

We know a great deal about Hildegard, because she was so creative in all the arts. Recently her music has become quite popular and is sold on disc. She lived to the ripe age of 80. Even so it is amazing just how much Hildegard managed to do in her lifetime. She was an unusual lady, very excitable and energetic. Yet she loved to spend time in prayer, and it is said she had many mystical experiences. That means she could feel God's presence very close to her, and it was said she could foresee the future. She lived in rather troubled times for the Church, so it was not surprising that she had long letters from four popes who asked for her advice. She also kept in touch with two emperors, and with King Henry II of England and St Bernard of Clairvaux.

Many women joined Hildegard in her Benedictine convent, and so she had a larger one built in Bingen. It was there, amongst the vineyards on the banks of the River Rhine, that she composed many of her poems, praising God for all living things. She composed her music, and wrote the lives of local saints, as well as two books on natural history. One of these was about the human body and all the illnesses and ailments that she had observed. This is one of the early medical books.

Some people found Hildegard a little strange, especially when she travelled across Germany visiting priests and important people, sharing with them her latest thoughts and ideas. One of her odd ideas was to invent her own language, a mixture of German and Latin, with its own peculiar alphabet. She did this as a pastime. We would call this lively lady an eccentric. But there was no doubt about her love of God and her tireless enthusiasm for sharing it with others. For this reason she is recognised as a saint in the Church, and regarded as one of the most powerful women of the Middle Ages.

THINK ABOUT IT
What part of creation would you like to sing about?

HILDEGARD DIED 1179

ISIDORE (SAINT)
FEAST DAY: 15 MAY

D. 1130

Isidore

Everyone has some connection with farmers. What is yours? Maybe you live in the countryside near a farm, and watch the tractors drive by. You may live on a farm and help feed the animals. If you live in a town you are still in touch with farmers, because every day you eat or drink what they send you. Almost everyone drinks milk from their cows, and eats eggs from their chickens. Your breakfast toast this morning had its beginning in a wheat field somewhere across the country. So perhaps we should all know a little about St Isidore, because he is the patron saint of farmers and agricultural workers.

It is quite surprising that Isidore was made a saint in the seventeenth century, because most saints were kings, archbishops, priests or nuns – and often important people from noble families. Isidore was only a humble farm labourer, who worked quietly and faithfully on his master's farm at Torrelaguna, near Madrid. He worked all his life for the same employer. Isidore married Maria and they had one son. Tragically the boy died, and the couple believed that God did not want them to have a family, but to put all their heart into living a prayerful life.

Isidore began each day by going to church before work. His master complained about his coming late. Isidore replied that serving his first master was more important. The farm owner could not be annoyed, because Isidore would make up the time, and served him with utmost honesty and hard work. He loved working in the fields with the plough, or the sickle. He could be alone and pray while he worked. People certainly noticed that he was a special person; they called it holiness.

When Isidore died, many stories were told about him, and his reputation for holiness spread across Spain. About 150 years after his death a biography was written about him, but some of the stories about him appear to be legend. For example, it was said that if he was late for work because he had been to Mass, the people saw angels working alongside him in the fields. Another story said that he gave away half of his grain to feed hungry birds, and the remaining half simply produced twice as much flour.

What is surely true is that he was a sincere worker, a very kind neighbour, and a fervent follower of Jesus. His wife was as good as her husband, and she is also looked upon as a saint in Spain. It was the Spanish King Philip III who asked the Church to canonise Isidore. The king was ill and he asked for the relics (bones) of Isidore to be brought into his bedroom. He recovered immediately, and so he told the Pope that Isidore had asked God to cure him. The Pope agreed that the farm labourer was a saint, and named him so.

THINK ABOUT IT
St Isidore got on quietly with every task he was given. Do you?

ISIDORE
DIED 1130

Jane Frances de Chantal (Saint)   D. 1641

FEAST DAY: 12 DECEMBER

Do you ever worry about things? Do you sometimes feel a bit sad and miserable because things aren't going too well? And do you sometimes not really know what you ought to do? Most people feel like this sometimes. St Jane Frances de Chantal was a worrier all her life, never really sure that she was doing the right thing. It has been suggested that she would make a really good patron saint for all of us. This is because she learnt to put up with her doubts and sadness, and show only kindness, sympathy and generosity to everyone around her.

Jane was born in Dijon, France, in the sixteenth century. Her father was the president of the parliament of Burgundy, so she was of noble family. At 20 she married Baron Christopher de Chantal of Bourbilly. He was a thoughtful and good husband and Jane loved him dearly. They had seven children, but only four survived. She suffered depression at the loss of her three babies, but never let this prevent her acting as a nobleman's wife. She entertained their guests with calm and dignity, and looked after the children and household without showing that her heart was sad and her mind uncertain. Someone described her as having 'the presence of a great lady, with intelligence and good humour too'.

After only eight years of marriage her beloved husband was killed in a hunting accident. Years of deep sadness followed. Living with a very difficult father-in-law did not help. Doctors today would say that she suffered an illness called 'clinical depression', and they would treat this with medication. Jane did not have that help. She turned to God instead. She decided not to marry again, but to learn to live a life of prayer. Most of the time she felt in the dark. When she prayed, she couldn't feel God listening to her, or being there at all.

Then Jane met St Francis de Sales, a local bishop. They became great friends, and he decided to take on the responsibility of guiding Jane's life. After the children grew up she thought she might become a Carmelite nun, but Francis had other ideas. He asked her to help him found a new religious order, less severe than was common at the time. It wasn't easy. Her family objected, and some of the women who joined her were rather fussy and difficult. But eventually the Order of the Visitation was founded, and Jane guided it with such skill that when she died there were 80 convents. At first the Church was not happy with the new Order, because Jane was accepting both women who were sick and widows. But she said simply, 'I like sick and sad people, I understand them.'

Jane learnt through her suffering how to live very close to God. Another saint who knew her was St Vincent de Paul. He said she was 'one of the holiest people I have ever met'.

THINK ABOUT IT
We don't always need a doctor, but we always need a friend.

JANE FRANCES
DE CHANTAL
DIED 1641

JANUSK KORCZAK
D. 1942
(JEWISH MARTYR OF THE HOLOCAUST)
POLISH DOCTOR

Janusk Korczak

Jesus of Nazareth was a Jewish boy, and as he grew up he learnt from the Jewish Scriptures, and from his teachers, that God wanted people to love everyone. When Jesus became a preacher that was the message he spread. He said that the greatest commandment was 'to love your neighbour as you love yourself'. Now that sounds quite an easy thing to do. Until you try it. It means that you would like everyone to have what *you* would like to have. Most of us want to have a bit more than our neighbour. Have you never wanted to have better trainers than your friends? Or have you never wanted to get the newest computer game before anyone else – just to show off a bit?

Unfortunately that is how human beings often behave, even world leaders. Wars are usually started because leaders want their country to be bigger or better than their neighbours. They don't want their neighbours to have what they have. They don't love their neighbours as much as they love themselves. Janusk Korczak was the victim of one of these wars.

Like Jesus, Janusk was a Jew. He was born in Poland about 1900 years after Jesus. When he grew up he became a doctor, and chose to look after the poor of his neighbourhood in Poland. He was especially concerned about the number of orphaned children because of war. He ran two orphanages, one for Jewish children and one for non-Jewish children. In 1939 Germany invaded Poland. It was the beginning of the Second World War in Europe. Germany was led by Adolf Hitler, who was building up the Nazi Party to help him produce a 'Master Race'.

Hitler had grown up as a Christian, a follower of Jesus. But he had never accepted that we should love our neighbour as we love ourselves. He wanted his own people to be the best and the most powerful. He decided to get rid of all the Jews, and any others whom he considered as 'inferior human beings'. This produced what is known as the 'Holocaust' – the killing of six million Jews in concentration camps. Hitler's secret police (the Gestapo) hunted out Jewish families and sent them off on countless trains, to camps where they were gassed to death.

When Hitler's Nazis took over Poland, some friends of Doctor Korczak offered to get him out of the country. But he refused to leave his Jewish orphans. In 1942, he and his staff, together with all 200 children, were marched three miles to the deportation train. He led them, holding two children's hands in his. They were all gassed at a death camp called Treblinka. This kind and courageous man gave up his life for the children. He firmly believed that all of us are loved as the children of God. And, like Jesus, he believed that no person, and no race, is better than another person or race.

THINK ABOUT IT
Try to love your neighbour in the same way as you love yourself.

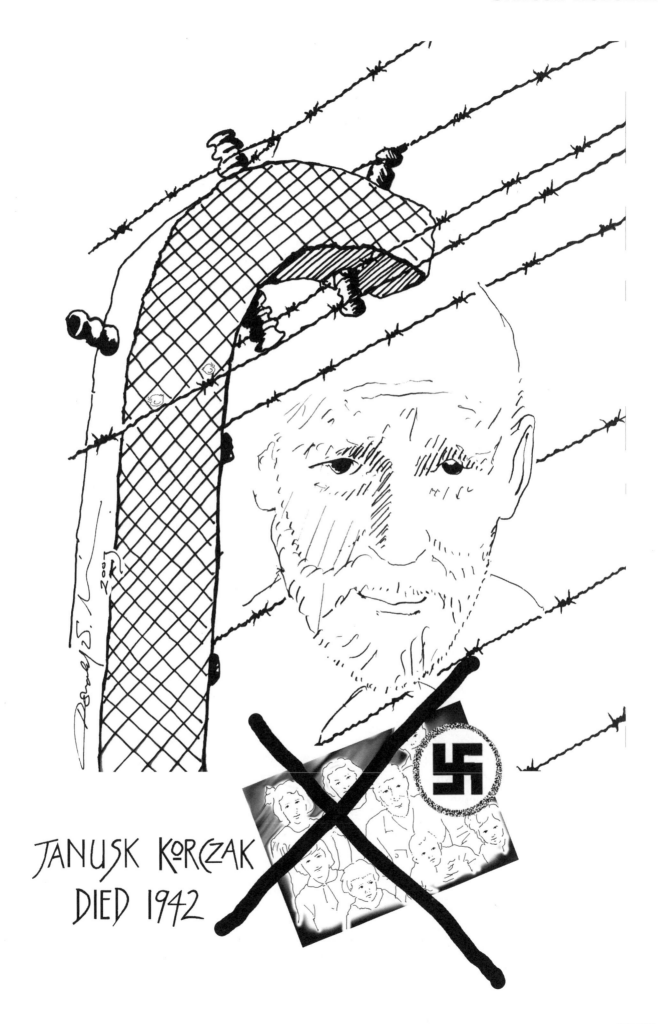

JANUSK KORCZAK
DIED 1942

Jean Vanier (vertical text)

JEAN VANIER (CHRISTIAN)   B. 1928
FOUNDER OF L'ARCHE COMMUNITIES

Many children and adults suffer from physical handicaps, or disabilities as they are sometimes called. They are not able to do some of the things that are generally taken for granted. Many children cannot walk because they once stepped on a land mine. Some children are born blind. These physical handicaps are visible, and most people respond with help and encouragement. However, as someone once wrote, 'It is much more difficult if the handicap is not visible. People more easily accept someone who acts normally but is without a limb, than someone who looks fine but acts strangely.' She was talking about mental handicap.

Jean Vanier is a man who decided to do something about this. He is a French Canadian who once served in the Canadian navy and then became a lecturer in philosophy in Toronto. Jean happened to be in France at the end of the Second World War, and saw the surviving victims of the Buchenwald concentration camp. He was distressed to see how many of them were more injured in their minds than in their bodies. Some years later, back in France, a Dominican priest took him to visit a mental asylum. He was shocked at the conditions, and could not believe that the patients (whom he calls intellectually disabled) needed to be shut away out of sight.

In 1964 Jean invited two of the patients, Philippe and Raphael, to live with him in an old house he had bought in the village of Trosly-Breuil. A few people joined them to make the house into a more homely place. The little group worked, prayed and laughed together, with everyone joining in. This was the beginning of a movement called L'Arche. It is named after Noah's Ark, which was a sign of life and hope. The rainbow is a sign of God's promise to be close to his people. Jean knew that God was especially close to people with handicaps. He loved to pray and read the Gospels, and he knew that Jesus welcomed everyone, especially those who were outcasts because of their diseases or disabilities.

Jean Vanier has spent the last 40 years building new L'Arche communities, and giving talks about the way we should welcome mentally handicapped people, and listen to what they can teach us. Today there are over 100 L'Arche communities across the world. There are a few in Britain. These communities are very different from hospitals or homes for people with mental handicap, where staff 'look after' patients. In Jean Vanier's homes there are no patients, because everyone is treated as part of a family. They simply live with one another – those with a handicap and those who want to share their lives with them. The members are from all Christian traditions, all faiths and all nationalities. Jesus would be very much at home in L'Arche!

THINK ABOUT IT
Everyone has a handicap (something they can't do).
What is yours?

JEAN VANIER

BORN 1928

John Vianney

JOHN VIANNEY (SAINT)   D. 1859
FEAST DAY: 4 AUGUST

If you find school work difficult, and don't get very good marks, then St John Vianney is the saint for you. He was usually bottom of the class. John was born in France at Dardilly in 1786. He was the son of a country farmer, and even as a boy wanted to be a priest. It was quite a struggle. He found Latin very difficult to learn during his training to be a priest, and kept failing his exams. It took him nine years of study instead of six. During this time he also hid for over a year in order to avoid going into the army. The bishop was doubtful about making him a priest, but decided that his determination and his obvious goodness were a better qualification.

When he was ordained a priest, John was sent to a small and neglected parish called Ars-en-Dombes. The bishop thought that he would be able to manage the small community. He was unprepared for what actually happened. John, now called the Curé of Ars, remained in the little village until his death, 40 years later. He never left there, but thousands of people went to the village to see him. In fact, so many people flocked there that a special booking office for Ars had to be set up in Lyons Station. At least 300 people a day were travelling out to visit him. Why was this?

When John arrived in his parish, there were hardly any people going to church. Within a very short time the entire population of the village, 230 people, were attending Mass and seeking private talks (confession) with their priest. He had the most extraordinary gift for helping people, and for preaching. His words about obeying God's commandments were strict, even quite severe. But his concern for people was kindness itself. He spoke gently to them, and seemed to understand the needs of all of them – even before they had time to tell him about themselves.

His fame quickly grew, and because he would turn no one away, he ended up spending nearly 18 hours daily in the 'confessional' (the private tiny room where people talk to their priest, and 'confess' or admit their sins to God). Some of the local priests were worried about the Curé of Ars, and called him ignorant or mad. But the bishop said, 'I wish, gentlemen, that all my clergy had the same kind of madness.'

The priests had misjudged John because they could not understand how anyone could have no time for themselves. John only had one meal a day, and often that was just a plate of potatoes. If he did take an hour off from the people who came to him, it was to rescue abandoned children. He once asked a neighbour to take one of these children in. The neighbour said, 'Sorry, we have no bed.' John replied, 'There's always yours.' John was often worn out, especially after spending hours each day at prayer. Three times he tried to leave and hide in a monastery. But he realised that people needed his care. The unlikely priest had become the example and patron saint for priests.

THINK ABOUT IT
You don't need to pass exams to become a kind and generous person.

JOHN VIANNEY
DIED 1859

KATHARINE DREXEL (SAINT)　　D. 1955
FEAST DAY: 3 MARCH

If you won the lottery, what would you do with the money? Katharine Drexel didn't need to buy a lottery ticket because she inherited millions of dollars from her father's estate. She gave it all away to help the poor. Katharine's father was a world-renowned banker from Philadelphia, Pennsylvania. He and her stepmother provided Katharine and her two sisters with a wonderful home that had every comfort. But they also wanted their children to share their good fortune with others. Two days every week Mrs Drexel opened the house to the poor. Food and clothing were distributed, and people in need were given help with their rent or other bills.

Mr Drexel once took Katharine on a trip to the north-west territories of the United States. Both were horrified by the poverty of the Native Americans, and by the way they were deprived of civil rights. Katharine was deeply affected by what she had seen, and determined that she would do something about it. But family tragedy struck. Her father died soon after the trip, and her mother fell ill with cancer. Katharine had to stay at home to look after her until she died. The three sisters inherited the family fortunes. Katharine knew what to do with her 20 million dollars: give it to the Native Americans.

But Katharine was not sure how she was going to organise this. She had always wanted to join a convent where she could spend her days in quiet prayer. On a journey to Rome she met Pope Leo XIII, and his words made her realise that she should become a missionary to the Native Americans. She could provide them with the schools that the Government denied them. In 1891 Katharine founded a religious congregation called the Sisters of the Blessed Sacrament. She went to Dakota and became friends with a Sioux chieftain, who helped her understand his people.

The Sisters organised a long-term plan to build a network of schools, churches and other facilities for Native Americans. Over the years their schools and mission centres spread across America. Katharine upset the Government in southern states by employing black teachers, and was threatened by the racist Ku Klux Klan for having mixed races in mission churches. She financed Xavier University in New Orleans for black students. Today it sends more graduates to medical school than any other university in America.

In 1935, when Katherine was 78 years old she suffered a severe heart attack. She had to retire quietly and leave the younger nuns to organise her congregation. At last she could spend her days in prayer, as she had always wanted. When she died, 20 years later, she left behind 500 nuns and 63 schools. Pope John Paul II proclaimed her a saint in 2000.

THINK ABOUT IT
Could you give all your winnings away?

Katharine Drexel

KATHARINE DREXEL
DIED 1955

MARGUERITE D'YOUVILLE (SAINT)   D. 1771

FEAST DAY: 23 DECEMBER

What do you know about Canada? It is known for its Rocky Mountains, ice hockey, red-coated Mounties, the Toronto Jays baseball team, the tall CP tower, the Niagara Falls, wide spaces, lakes, forests and French Quebec. Marguerite D'Youville was born in Quebec 300 years ago. She was a happy child, always smiling. She was very sad, however, when her father died when she was only 13 years old. She left school, which she really liked, to help her mother. Her family had very little money and life became very difficult. From that time on, Marguerite had to cope with one disaster after another. Somehow she faced them all with courage and her warm smile.

When she was just 21 years old, Marguerite married a handsome young fur trader, François D'Youville. It was a great mistake, because he turned out to be completely unfaithful to her, and he wasted all his family's fortune. He was utterly selfish, with no concern for others. He even got Native Americans drunk so that he could steal the little they had. Of the six babies the young couple had, only two survived.

It was during this very difficult marriage that Marguerite had an experience that she could never quite describe. She just knew, with a great certainty, that God loved her as a Father, and that he would make life happy for her, just as her earthly father had done when she was a child. She knew she could put up with her difficult husband, and her unkind mother-in-law, because she felt so loved by God. Even so, Marguerite must have been relieved when François died after only eight years of the marriage. She had no doubt what she had to do – spend the rest of her life caring for those worse off than herself in Montreal.

Over the next few years, she raised money and organised help for the homeless and the poor in the city. Gradually others joined in to help her, and she was able to rent a house for the most needy. When the house burnt down it would have been easy to give up. But not Marguerite. She knelt in the ashes and prayed her usual prayer of thanksgiving to God, the *Te Deum*. It was the moment that she knew that she and her companions must ask the bishop to accept them as a new religious community. He called them the Sisters of Charity. They became known as the Grey Sisters because of the colour of their dress, and today they work for the destitute throughout the world, including the Inuit people of North America.

It is amazing that Marguerite never lost trust in God's love for her. She had so many difficulties: her father's early death; the poverty that it brought; a disastrous marriage; the death of four babies; a dreadful mother-in-law; constant criticism and mockery for working with destitute people and drunkards; and finally fire and bankruptcy. Pope John Paul II recognised her smile as the smile of a saint.

THINK ABOUT IT
Try to manage a smile when life is tough. It helps.

MARGUERITE D'YOUVILLE DIED 1771

Martha

MARTHA (SAINT) FIRST CENTURY
FEAST DAY: 29 JULY (WEST); 6 JUNE (EAST)

'I always have to do the washing-up. It's not fair. Why can't she help?' Ever heard that before? I expect children in every family argue about doing more jobs than the others. Who seems to get off lightly in your family? St Luke tells a story about a family of Jesus' friends living in Bethany, a town near Jerusalem. There were two sisters, Mary and Martha, and their brother Lazarus.

Luke doesn't tell us very much about their early lives. He tells us enough about Mary and Martha for us to guess that when they were younger they argued, like you do! The famous story that Luke tells is about a visit Jesus made to their house. It is quite a walk out to Bethany, so Jesus was probably tired when he arrived and he was welcomed indoors by Martha. She would have washed the dust off his feet and told him to sit and rest. Then she bustled off to the kitchen to prepare a good meal.

Meanwhile Mary, the quiet one, went and sat with Jesus to listen to all he had to say. Martha was a bit fed up that her sister didn't offer to help in the kitchen, so she popped her head round the door, and complained to Jesus. 'Lord, aren't you bothered that Mary leaves me to do all the work out here? Tell her to come and give me a hand.' To her surprise, Jesus told her, 'Martha, Martha, do stop worrying. You're getting troubled about so many things, when only one thing is necessary. Mary has the right idea, and she can stay here.' We are not told the end of the story. How do you think Martha felt?

Christians have thought about Luke's story of the sisters. It is very often used as a symbol of two ways of serving God. Some people, like Mary, choose to get close to Jesus and his Father by spending many hours in prayer. They are thinkers, and we call them contemplatives. But Martha represents all those Christians who are busy working to provide for others – teachers providing education, nurses providing health care, nuns in religious congregations that care for the destitute and for people who are disadvantaged. In the Gospel story it is unlikely that Luke had this in mind. He may have meant that Martha was making a big fuss over a meal with too many dishes, when one simple one would have done. People can make this mistake when they have guests.

St John tells us two more stories about the sisters. In one, Lazarus had died and Jesus brought him back to life, but not before the worried Martha complained that after four days his body would smell. In the other story Jesus again visited the Bethany home, and once more it was Martha who prepared the meal while Mary took some precious oils and poured them over Jesus' feet. From these stories we can tell that Martha was a busy lady who cared about greeting her friends. John tells us that Jesus 'loved Martha and her sister and Lazarus'. It isn't surprising that the Church calls Martha a saint and the patron of cooks and mums in the kitchen. Does your mother know that?

THINK ABOUT IT
Do the washing-up without being asked.

MARTHA

DIED 1ST CENTURY

MARTIN LUTHER KING   D. 1968
(PASTOR AND CIVIL RIGHTS LEADER)
REMEMBERED ON THE THIRD MONDAY IN JANUARY

Martin Luther King

One day a young black American boy and his father went into a shop to buy shoes. But the shopkeeper refused to serve them because they were sitting in seats reserved for white people only. That was the moment when the boy decided he would spend his life working for equal rights for all Americans. He became a Baptist minister (pastor) like his father, Martin Luther King Senior.

Martin Luther Junior was born in Atlanta, Georgia, in 1929. The black Americans in the South were descendants of the four million African slaves shipped to America centuries earlier. Although Abraham Lincoln had stopped the slavery in 1865, Martin Luther King's people were still treated like slaves, and were denied many of the rights of white people. They had poorer housing and education, and in some states were not allowed to vote. White and black Americans were kept separate in schools, restaurants, hotels and bars. They could not even use the same transport.

The younger Martin Luther King began his ministry as a pastor in Montgomery, the state capital of Alabama, around the same time that he married Coretta Scott. He arrived in 1954, at the same time as a man called Malcolm X, leader of the 'Black Power Movement', was calling on people to use violence in order to bring about equal rights. The pastor wanted to 'fight' for equal human rights, but only in a peaceful way. He organised non-violent protests.

Pastor King told his supporters that they should follow the example of Gandhi in India, by marching in peaceful protest. He preached that this might well mean suffering and sacrifice, as it had done for Jesus. Life did become frightening for the pastor and his young family. By 1960 his appeals for equal rights developed into the 'Civil Rights Movement'. As the leader of the movement, he was recognised everywhere. His family received death threats; his house was bombed; he was stabbed, stoned and imprisoned. Yet he never stopped preaching peace and forgiveness. Some white people knew he was right, and he was awarded the Nobel Peace Prize in 1964.

Gradually things improved for black Americans, especially following the 1965 peace march in Montgomery. The police were violent in breaking it up with tear gas and clubs, and it shocked the millions who saw it on television. Almost immediately the Government passed a Voting Rights Act, giving equal rights to all Americans. Tragically the peace-loving pastor did not live to enjoy the success. Only three years later he was killed by a white man, James Earl Ray. He was only 39 years old. In his last sermon he had said: 'If any of you are around when I die . . . I want you to say that I tried to love and serve humanity.' In doing this he was loving and serving God too.

THINK ABOUT IT
All people are equal in God's eyes. Are they in yours?

MARTIN
LUTHER
KING
B·1929·
D·1968·

Mary Ramabai

MARY RAMABAI (PANDITA) D. 1922
COMMEMORATED BY THE ANGLICAN CHURCH ON 30 APRIL

It was said of Mary Ramabai that 'she wished to fly with the swallows and soar with the lark' in the open sky. In other words, she always wanted to be free to do the things she loved. She was born in 1858 in India, when freedom was still a dream for many women – especially for her, because her family were Hindu, her father being a learned Brahmin, which made him important and respected. But he was to bring her up in an unusual way.

He believed in educating girls. In India, 150 years ago, this was unheard of. He taught Ramabai to read, and she quickly understood the Hindu Scriptures. But her happy childhood was shattered when, in the course of a great famine, her parents and her sister died. Her father's last words to her were: 'Remember, you are my youngest, most beloved child; I have given you into the hands of God. You are his, and to him alone you must belong, and serve him all your life.'

That is exactly what Ramabai did. She and her brother were cared for by Anglican missionaries, in Calcutta. It was there that she was asked to teach some women's groups their duties according to Hindu Scripture and law. She found it difficult because, according to this law, women were inferior to men. Women could only reach freedom from long cycles of reincarnation by serving their husbands blindly. Ramabai disagreed with this, and set up her own lectures in the university. She spoke of her opposition to the caste system which said that people were not all equal. She also opposed child marriages. It was at this time that she was given the Hindu title of respect, Pandita.

Ramabai married when she was 22 years old and had a daughter, Monorama, but her husband died of typhoid a year later. She moved to Poona, and met the Anglican Wantage Sisters. They changed her life. With her little daughter she moved to England, and the nuns arranged for her to study at Cheltenham Ladies' College. Ramabai was so impressed by the nuns' work that she was baptised into the Church of England, taking the name Mary. However, she was an unusual Christian and worried the nuns by her refusal to accept that by being in one denomination she was not free to explore others. She decided to follow the Christian Gospel, but had little time for any of the rules or teaching that kept Christians divided.

Eventually, after studying and teaching both in England and America, Mary Ramabai returned to India. There she set up schools for the poorest Indian girls, child widows and unwanted wives and daughters. In her spare time she translated the Bible into her own Indian language. Today, 80 years after her death, many Christians are able to admire her free spirit and her refusal to accept divisions, both racial and religious.

THINK ABOUT IT
If you have a chance, make friends with someone from another race or religion.

MARY RAMABAI
DIED 1922

Mary Slessor

MARY SLESSOR (MISSIONARY)

D. 1915

COMMEMORATED BY THE ANGLICAN CHURCH ON 11 JANUARY

If you ever visit Dundee and go to the museum, you will find a display about a lady they call the 'Saint of Dundee' and the 'White Queen of Okoyong'. Who is this lady? She is Mary Slessor. She came from a poor Christian family in Aberdeen, Scotland. Her father, a shoemaker, drank so heavily that he could not keep his job. So the family moved to Dundee for her mother to find a job in the textile mills.

When she was only 11, Mary joined her mother for six hours' work each day. She spent another six hours each day in the mill school. Sunday was the day she loved best. It was a relief from the hard work, and a joy to listen to the exciting stories she heard at church. She could sit in the bench at the Presbyterian church and imagine places far away. Her church had sent missionaries to Calabar in West Africa, and they would sometimes return to talk about their dangerous work there. Back at home the Slessor children played at being missionaries and preached to their dolls.

When Mary was a teenager she began to take her missionary dreams seriously. An over-strict woman had warned her and her friends that people would go to hell if they didn't believe in Jesus. So Mary set her heart on going out to Nigeria to tell them about Jesus. She had to work for another 14 years in the mill to support the family. She taught herself by propping up her books on the loom as she worked. Eventually, aged 27, she left for Calabar, to preach the Gospel to the people described as the most dangerous in Nigeria. They had been ruined by white slave masters, who bought them with gin and rum. Everyone feared for Mary's safety.

But she was amazing. She quickly learnt the Efik language and began to visit the tribal chiefs. She talked to them with confidence, persuading them to listen to her ideas about God, and about how to behave. She was sent to work amongst a fierce tribe called the Okoyong. They had horrible practices, like sacrificing human beings and killing second-born twins. Mary determined to save these lives. She started an orphanage for twins, and faced the tribal chiefs with courage. She even hit one over the head with her umbrella. The people found her just and sensible, and lovable.

The British Government made her their official representative to the Okoyong people. She became their magistrate and used her own common sense to solve their arguments. She organised their trade. Even the tribal chiefs accepted her authority, and changed their bad laws. She died in Nigeria and was buried with her beloved tribe. They called her *Eka kpukru owo*, which means 'everyone's mother'. The former mill girl, who had been taught about a fierce and punishing God, had learnt to teach others about a compassionate and loving God.

THINK ABOUT IT
It's easier to talk to people if you love them.

MARY SLESSOR DIED 1915

MONICA (SAINT)

D. 387

FEAST DAY: 27 AUGUST

Monica

Mothers can be very trying at times, because they worry too much. 'Have you got your lunch box?' 'Wrap up warm.' 'You need your sleep, get to bed now.' Mothers only keep on because they love their children so much. You would soon be worried if your mum stopped the nagging, and just ignored you instead.

There is one very famous nagging mother called Monica. Although she lived centuries ago, we know about her because her eldest son, Augustine, wrote about her in a book called *Confessions*. Monica had been brought up as a Christian in North Africa, and married when she was only 14 years old. Her husband Patricius, a pagan soldier, turned out to be difficult. He was bad-tempered, often got drunk, and went with other women. He was not too pleased that Monica wanted to bring up their three children as Christians.

Augustine was not happy either. He was rather like his father. He went to Carthage to study and enjoyed the social life. Monica worried because he had made friends with a crowd that got him in trouble. He hung around with a woman his mother disapproved of, and joined a strange religious group called the Manichaeans. Christians called them heretics. His mother wept over him and his wild ways. But she was also confident that goodness would win through. Even her unfaithful husband became a Christian just before he died, when she was 40 years old.

Augustine got tired of his student friends, and moved to Rome with his partner and their child. Monica insisted on going with them. Augustine gave her the wrong time of the boat's departure, and she was left behind. But she was determined to see her son succeed by marrying into wealth, and becoming a Christian. She followed him from city to city. Eventually friends, including Bishop Ambrose of Milan, told her to stop worrying her son, and leave him to work out his own life.

But mothers never give up. Monica stopped arguing and turned to prayer instead, asking God again and again to help her son understand Christianity. Imagine her surprise and joy when Augustine decided to become not only a Christian but also a priest. While he studied she stayed with him, as his housekeeper. On the journey back to North Africa after his baptism, Monica caught a fever. A few days later she died. She never knew her son was to become one of Christianity's most outstanding bishops.

THINK ABOUT IT
When your mother nags, it's only because she loves you.

OCTAVIA HILL (SOCIAL REFORMER)

D. 1912

COMMEMORATED BY THE ANGLICAN CHURCH ON 13 AUGUST

Octavia Hill

If Octavia Hill lived today she would probably work for Help the Homeless or Shelter. She would perhaps speak out about environmental issues and campaign for keeping footpaths open. She might be a member of the Green Party. But she lived a century ago in Victorian London, and had to work in different ways. She was inspired by her deep faith in God and her humble, quiet love for the poor.

In the nineteenth century it was difficult for the poor to survive. Octavia Hill knew this because her mother had struggled to bring up five daughters alone. Octavia became a teacher, and when she visited her pupils' families she was shocked by the conditions they lived in. London was overcrowded and families lived in slums. (She refused to call them this.) She turned to the Christian Socialists for help. The artist John Ruskin helped her buy three run-down dwellings, so that she could offer rooms to the poor. She believed that if she taught the families to respect and look after the property, they would become happier in their neglected environment.

Octavia treated each family as special. She often sat down with them to show them how to use their little money wisely. She was the first person to introduce the rights and duties of landlord and tenant. Her work grew and she took on more properties, including some owned by the Church. She set up training centres in housing management in other English cities, and then her work spread to Holland, Germany and the United States. This meant many meetings with committees and politicians, but Octavia preferred working more quietly with the poor themselves. From them she learnt what was really best for them.

She tried to prevent the Government building high-rise flats simply for profit, insisting that the small dwelling gave privacy, a back yard for an invalid chair, a swing for children, a shed for a workshop, and space for creepers and bulbs. It was this awareness of people's human needs that made her a great social reformer. She advised the Government to open up the parks and squares to the public, and build public footpaths. She successfully called for a 'Green Belt' around cities. Her last task was rescuing a river from becoming a rubbish tip.

Octavia never married, she was too busy helping the poor. But she never spoke to them about her love for God which was her inspiration, and was angry with priests who gave to the poor simply to get them into church. She spent her life joyfully – singing the Magnificat on her walks, preparing parties for her tenants and planting daises around their dwellings. She wished she could tell people how much she loved them. But she was too shy. It was just like her to refuse the suggestion that she should be buried in Westminster Abbey.

THINK ABOUT IT
Helping others is best done without broadcasting it.

OCTAVIA HILL
DIED 1912

OSCAR ROMERO (BISHOP AND MARTYR)

D. 1980

REMEMBERED ON 24 MARCH

Do you know the names of any bishops? Who is the Archbishop of Canterbury? Which bishop (called a Cardinal) is the head of the Catholic Church in England and Wales? Who is the bishop of your diocese? A diocese is the region that is looked after by a bishop in the Church. One Catholic bishop, who died not so long ago, is well known. A statue of him has even been put up on the front of Westminster Abbey, which is a Church of England place of worship. So why is he important?

He is called Archbishop Oscar Romero, and he was born in El Salvador, a country in Central America. Oscar came from a simple Catholic family that was able to send him to school. Many of their neighbours never had enough money for education. Oscar enjoyed studying and worked very hard. He was keen to become a priest, and was sent to Rome for his studies. After he was ordained, he returned to live a fairly comfortable life as a parish priest, and then as a bishop.

El Salvador is a country where the land is owned by just a few very rich families. The rest are desperately poor, and the rich are not keen to share with their poor neighbours. Bishop Romero was eventually made the archbishop of the capital city, San Salvador. This meant that he could have lived an even more comfortable life, in a fine house as a friend of the rich. It is a sad fact that until then the official Church protected the wealthy and successful families.

But in 1968 the bishops of South and Central America met together to take a fresh look at the Gospel. They found that it spoke of a Jesus who sided with the poor. Against great opposition from the Government and some important members of the Church, many nuns and priests began to speak up for the rights of the poor. When Archbishop Romero supported them and spoke out against the selfishness and injustice of people who were rich and powerful, he was in deep trouble.

The archbishop told his wealthy countrymen and women to share what they had with the rest of the country, especially with those who had least. He said that this is what was demanded by the Gospel. He was told to be quiet. But he continued to remind the politicians to work for all the people of their country. One day, while he was saying Mass, government soldiers came into the church and shot him dead. The poor were heartbroken at losing the bishop who, like Jesus, had been on their side. Christians have recognised him as a martyr, who died because he was following the example of Jesus.

THINK ABOUT IT
Is there something you can give to someone worse off than yourself?

OSCAR ROMERO
DIED 1980

PETER CLAVER (SAINT)   D. 1654
FEAST DAY: 9 SEPTEMBER

Peter Claver

Some holy people do things that we find quite strange. St Peter Claver's life was an odd mixture of extreme kindness and extreme violence. But the violence was always against himself.

Peter was born in Spain and studied to become a Jesuit priest on the island of Majorca. The college porter was Alphonsus Rodriguez, also later canonised as a saint. He urged the young, nervous student to leave Europe and go to the Indies, to save the millions of slaves being deported there from Africa. He could work in New Grenada, now called Colombia. Peter did as he advised, and was eventually ordained priest in Cartagena, the northern port of Colombia, and the centre of the South American slave trade. Thousands of West African slaves arrived each year, to live in terrible conditions.

Fr Peter vowed that he would be 'the slave of the African slaves for ever'. And he was. For the next 40 years, relentlessly, day and night, he met them in the ships, bringing food, tobacco, brandy and medicines. He bathed their festering wounds, and buried the many who had died on the journey. The stench of the slave ships in the dock was almost unbearable. Few people had the courage to go below deck into the dark bowels of the ships, but Fr Peter moved among the slaves, living, dying and dead, with extraordinary kindness. He said that it was no use talking about Jesus until he had acted like him. Eventually he was able to share the Gospel of Jesus with the slaves, and baptised more than 300,000 of them.

If Fr Peter was kindness itself to the wretched slaves, especially those who were wounded, he was violently hard on himself. Although he found the smell so awful, and often the sights so ugly, that he was physically sick, he was ashamed of himself and would bend down and kiss the slaves' open sores. He continued to be very hard on himself, even hitting his own body to feel the pain that his slaves felt. He visited the slaves as they worked in mines and on plantations, and visited jails to comfort the prisoners, white and black. It is surprising that he lived to be 74 years old. His last four years were spent in isolation and in constant pain, abandoned except for a servant who often neglected him. The servant was one of his African slaves.

St Peter Claver has been criticised for not condemning slavery. He left that to other saintly people who tried to change the system. Peter simply showed love to each outcast that came his way. Rather like Jesus in the Gospel.

THINK ABOUT IT
Jesus said: 'Whatever you do to the least of my brothers and sisters, you do to me.'

PETER CLAVER

DIED 1654

PIERRE TOUSSAINT (CANDIDATE FOR SAINTHOOD)

D. 1853

REMEMBERED ON 30 JUNE

St Patrick's Catholic Cathedral is on the famous Fifth Avenue in New York. In a vault under the sanctuary, alongside the tombs of archbishops of New York, stands the tomb of Pierre Toussaint, a slave who died 150 years ago. The people of New York are praying that he will one day be recognised as the patron saint of their city.

Pierre's great-grandmother was sold into slavery in Africa, and taken to the island of Haiti, off the coast of Central America, a French colony with rich sugar and coffee plantations. The plantation owners were French, and the slaves worked in terrible conditions in their fields. The Toussaints were sold as slaves to the Bérard family, where Pierre became a House Boy. They were lucky. Their master was a kind man, who trusted them and treated them with dignity.

Young Pierre was a happy and popular boy. He loved music and dancing, and singing calypso-style in the Creole language. The Bérards taught him to read, write and play the violin. He grew to love this generous family, and eventually adopted their Catholic faith. Then disaster struck. The French Revolution in Paris had made a Declaration of the Rights of Man, which demanded the freedom of slaves. When the selfish French plantation owners in Haiti refused to act, their slaves revolted. Many owners, including the Bérards, had to leave. They settled in New York, taking Pierre with them as a servant. They had him trained as a hairdresser.

Things did not go well. Monsieur Bérard died of TB on a return visit to Haiti. The property there had been destroyed and his New York business failed. His heartbroken wife was left destitute. So young Pierre, working as a hairdresser, decided to give his wages to his mistress. Over the next years he became the most popular hairdresser to the rich white ladies of New York. He repaid his kind mistress by inviting her friends to parties. He provided the food himself, but acted in public as her servant.

Pierre married Juliette, a former slave, and adopted the baby daughter of his sister. He took her with him on his visits to the sick, the dying, and the poor immigrants. He earned a good salary, but gave most of it away. He and Juliette took in abandoned slave children and gave them an education. They even built an orphanage for white children. He gave much of his money to build up the Catholic community. Yet on one occasion he was turned away from St Patrick's Cathedral for being black! Today's New Yorkers know better. They love this dignified man, who gave generously to everyone, treating them all equally, because 'they are loved by God'.

THINK ABOUT IT
We are happy when we make other people happy.

Pierre Toussaint

RIGOBERTA MENCHU (CHAMPION FOR JUSTICE)

B. 1959

LOVED AND ADMIRED BY THE POOR IN CENTRAL AMERICA

Rigoberta Menchu

When the 1992 Nobel Peace Prize was announced, very few people had ever heard of the winner. It was Rigoberta Menchu, a Mayan Indian *campesina* (country woman) from Guatemala, in Central America. She never went to school, and until she was 19 years old she could only speak her local K'iche language, not spoken anywhere else in the world. Her family were migrant workers, and she had found work as a maid. Rigoberta won the prize for her astonishing work to improve the lives of her people.

The young *campesina* was given courage and inspiration by her Catholic parish, which was looked after by Spanish Sacred Heart Fathers. They encouraged both men and women to learn Spanish, which would give them better opportunities for work, and the means to speak out to the larger world beyond their villages. The priests trained Rigoberta to be a parish catechist. A catechist teaches others about their faith, and sometimes takes services when the priest is away. Everyone in the village recognised Rigoberta as a strong and courageous leader.

The Mayan people were violently oppressed by the Government and military of Guatemala. In 1979, Rigoberta's 16-year-old brother Petrocinio was tortured and burnt alive in front of his family. Then her father Vincente, a union leader, was also killed. Three months later her mother was treated violently and slowly put to death while a soldier prevented the villagers from helping her. In 1981, hunted by the army, Rigoberta went into exile in Mexico. Encouraged by Maryknoll nuns, who admired her deep faith, she found ways of telling the world about the injustices against Indigenous People (people who originally owned the land).

Rigoberta organised resistance to the Guatemala regime, urging her Indian peasants to oppose the injustices. Through her life story, *I, Rigoberta Menchu*, and a film about the situation in her country, she became known in the West as a powerful voice for Indian rights and for reconciliation between ethnic groups. Since receiving the Nobel Prize, she has been an Ambassador for the United Nations, and continues to be an adviser to them today on behalf of all Indigenous People.

Rigoberta believes that the Kingdom of God must begin on earth. It is not something we must wait for until after death. She says, 'I learned, from suffering, what it is to be a committed Christian. It is to condemn injustices against people.' There are many Christians, like Rigoberta, who pray: 'Thy kingdom come on earth, as it is in heaven.'

THINK ABOUT IT
You can do what seems impossible, if you really want it.

RIGOBERTA MENCHU
B□1959

SEAN DEVEREUX
(VOLUNTEER WORKER IN AFRICA)

D. 1993

KILLED IN SOMALIA WORKING FOR UNICEF

Sean Devereux

What is your favourite lesson in school? Maths? English? Geography? If it is PE, you would certainly have enjoyed your lessons with Sean Devereux. Sean was a very popular PE teacher in a Surrey school. His pupils were sad when he decided to leave them to teach in the St Francis Salesian School in Liberia, West Africa. No one was surprised that he was changing a comfortable job for an uncomfortable one.

Sean and his two sisters were brought up in a loving and warm Irish Catholic home. His father worked for an airline company, so the family enjoyed wonderful holidays abroad. Sean loved Africa. He went to the Salesian College in Farnborough, where he became a very good athlete. He was full of fun and very popular at school. He was made the school captain. After Loughborough University, Sean went to teach at a Salesian school in Chertsey, and even thought of becoming a priest.

When Sean went to Liberia everyone, especially the 900 school children, immediately loved him. He sent his family charming videos of his daily routine, where happy children called him Mr Sean. He loved playing football with the boys, as well as spending quiet moments in the chapel. But his carefree days ended when in 1990 civil war broke out in Liberia. He was out of town organising a sports event when troops attacked, and he could never return to the school. To his dismay he heard that some of his boys had been forced into the army.

Sean joined the United Nations as a volunteer relief worker. With great courage he went to the front line of the fighting, and even argued with a crazy rebel leader to free one of his former pupils from the army. He worked with Salesian priests to look after child soldiers whose minds had been unbalanced by what they had seen. Once when he was beaten up by a drunken soldier, it was one of his pupils who rescued him. Sean angered the authorities because he was giving food to both sides of the conflict. He had to leave, and chose to go on a more dangerous mission to the war in Somalia. He joined UNICEF, the organisation working for children's rights.

It was there, working for a huge relief operation in Kismayo, that Sean spoke out against injustices that he saw. When journalists interviewed him on international television, he spoke honestly about the corruption. It cost him his life. He was shot to keep him quiet. His UNICEF friends were distraught that they had lost their best worker. At his funeral in England one of the priests said: 'Sean was one of the most courageous men I have ever known. He followed St John Bosco in his two ideals: to be a saint in shirt sleeves, and to serve the Lord with gladness.'

In Sean's short life he followed the Gospel, loving others and giving his life for them.

THINK ABOUT IT
Find out what you can about the work of UNICEF.

SEAN DEVEREUX
DIED 1993

BLESSED TERESA OF CALCUTTA D. 1997 (MISSIONARY)

ALREADY ACCLAIMED A SAINT BY THE PEOPLE

Mother Teresa is unique. Many people have heard about this Catholic nun, and most already think of her as a saint, even those who never go to church, or believe in God. Why is this? Mother Teresa became a world figure by appearing on television, meeting world leaders and shocking people into thinking about the poor.

Mother Teresa was born in Serbia in 1910, and baptised Agnes by her parents, who were grocers. She was a thoughtful girl, and listened carefully in church when her parish priest read letters from missionary priests in Calcutta, India. She decided to become a missionary herself. She was only 17 years old when she left for Dublin to train as a Loreto nun. As Sister Teresa, she was sent to India to teach geography at the smart St Mary's High School in Calcutta. She encouraged her pupils to help the poor around them, but eventually became uncomfortable in her comfortable surroundings.

Sister Teresa asked the Pope if she could leave the Loreto nuns and work for the poor. He agreed. She took a room in the slums and learnt a little about nursing, and was soon joined by a few of her old pupils. It was the beginning of a new religious congregation, called the Missionaries of Charity, and Teresa was given the title 'Mother'. The city gave her a disused building where she took in people who had been left to die on the streets. When her work was filmed by a television crew, Mother Teresa had a world-wide audience. Everyone would now recognise the little wrinkled nun, dressed in a white and blue sari.

The Missionaries of Charity live amongst the poor, and share their poverty. They possess nothing, eat very simply and travel by foot. The sisters spend several hours each day in prayer. For the rest of the day they attend the sick, visit poor families, comfort the dying and nurse lepers. Mother Teresa was always outspoken. Once, whilst on television, she told the President of the United States, face to face, that he was wrong not to defend unborn babies. She firmly believed that abortion is always wrong, and said she would always look after unwanted babies. Her sisters rescue many abandoned children.

By the time Mother Teresa died in 1997, four thousand sisters were working in 107 centres all over the world. Why is Mother Teresa recognised when so many other people also work for the poor? The modern media, television and the press, have helped. But perhaps it is because she did exactly what Jesus did – she treated every individual she met as special. She would spend hours with one person if she felt that person needed her care. She said, 'We often neglect the small things. We show our love of God by writing a letter, a short visit, carrying shopping for someone, or by a mere smile.'

THINK ABOUT IT
Do something small for someone today.

MOTHER TERESA
B · 1910 · D · 1997

THÉOPHANE VÉNARD (SAINT AND MARTYR)

D. 1861

FEAST DAY: 4 DECEMBER

Théophane Vénard

Not many people have heard of St Théophane Vénard. He is one of the new saints canonised by Pope John Paul II. He was only 32 years old when he died, and everyone who knew him agreed that he would always be remembered for his happy laugh. The Church said that he would also be remembered for his great love of God. That love is what made him so happy.

Jean-Théophane was born in Poitiers, France, in 1829. His family encouraged him to go to church and learn his catechism (the Church's teachings). When he was only 9 years old, he read about a priest from his town who had gone to Tonkin, in Vietnam (then called Indochina). People had objected to his preaching of Christianity and he was finally put to death. The church in Poitiers was calling him a martyr. Théophane got very excited and happily shouted out, 'Me too! I want to be a martyr!' His parents agreed that he could study for the priesthood, and when he was 12 years old, sent him to school in Douai. After years of school and seminary training he joined the Society of Foreign Missionaries in Paris. This worried his family: missionaries leaving the college were being killed for preaching the Gospel.

When he was 23 years old, Théophane was ordained a priest, and sent to Hong Kong to prepare for missionary work in China. But just like St Francis Xavier, who centuries before had prepared to set foot in mainland China, he never got there. His superiors changed their mind, and sent him to Indochina (Vietnam) instead. Théophane was quite happy, realising that his childhood dream of martyrdom in that land might come true.

Christians in Indochina at this time were still being persecuted, and the missionaries had to work in secret. For five years Théophane worked quietly with other priests looking after the thousands of new Christians. Eventually they had to go into hiding. The young French missionary, together with another priest and a bishop, were given refuge by an old lady, in her poor house. The three of them hid in a tiny dark space, only a few feet square, day and night for three weeks. Typically, Théophane sent a message to a friend saying, 'You would be quite scandalised at our jollity.'

They were betrayed by a visitor to the house, arrested and condemned to death. For two months Théophane was kept in a small cage. He was given permission to write to his father, and assured him that he was being treated well, without brutality. Even the mandarin (local leader) regretted the law that condemned him to death. With his usual joy, Théophane went to his execution on 2 February 1861.

THINK ABOUT IT
Loving God can make you very happy.

VLADIMIR OF KIEV (SAINT) D. 1015
FEAST DAY: 15 JULY

The story of St Vladimir of Kiev is like a history lesson. It may help you to have a map in front of you to follow his story.

Vladimir was a Viking. Do you remember the story of the Vikings? The people who lived in Scandinavia (Denmark, Norway and Sweden) were called Norsemen. They were farmers and fishermen. Norsemen who sailed abroad were called Vikings. They were warriors and adventurers. From the ninth century onwards, some of them sailed south-west and landed in England. A little later others sailed south-east and landed in Russia.

Vladimir the Viking was one of these raiders who sailed up the long rivers into the vast lands that were then ruled by Slavs. The Slav people had arrived from Europe 200 years earlier, and set up several separate kingdoms. The Vikings eventually settled in a Slav kingdom around Kiev. They called the area 'Rus'. It didn't happen smoothly, because Vladimir could be fierce, and had several fights with his own brothers on the way. Vladimir was made head of the State of Rus in 980.

At the time his land was the home of many different groups, separated by different religions and cultures. Vladimir wanted to unite his people by finding a common religion. He sent out envoys to report on the religions of neighbouring kingdoms. They reported that the ceremonies in Western Christianity were too simple, and that Islam was not exciting, especially as it forbade alcohol. When the envoy who had gone south described the colourful splendour of the Christian celebrations he had seen in Santa Sophia Cathedral in Constantinople, Vladimir went to look himself. He decided, 'That's the one.' Constantinople was the centre of the Byzantine Empire.

Vladimir was baptised a Christian and then married Anne, the daughter of the Byzantine emperor, Basil II. He loved Anne, but the marriage was also very convenient. He was able to make his nobles accept baptism too. Gradually the Rus kingdom became totally Christian. Over the centuries, when Rus and the kingdoms came closer together and the vast area was called Russia, it was the Christian faith that kept the people united. The Church in Russia developed its own style of the Eastern Byzantine Greek Church, with its onion-domed churches, decorated inside with icons and mosaic. The liturgy is always celebrated with music, in great dignity.

It could seem that Prince Vladimir was more of a political leader than a saintly man. But all the records show that he changed from a tough Viking warrior to a kind ruler, who provided for the poor, and pardoned murderers and thieves. That kind of leadership was unheard of in earlier kingdoms. It isn't surprising that St Vladimir of Kiev is the loved patron saint of the Russian people.

THINK ABOUT IT
It is possible to change bad habits for good ones.

VLADIMIR
OF KIEV

DIED 1015

Wang Zhiming

WANG ZHIMING (MARTYR)   D. 1973
REMEMBERED ON 29 DECEMBER

China is a country with a vast population, and a magnificent history of culture and civilisation, dating back 3000 years. But until very recently foreigners with different ideas were not welcome. Even so, a few Christian missionaries, Catholic and Protestant, did reach some provinces of China, and today a number of Christian Churches continue to be active there.

In the southern province of Yunnan, close to Vietnam, Christian missionaries settled near the end of the nineteenth century. They were allowed to stay, and by 1906 they had opened a new mission in a region called Wuding. Wang Zhiming was born at this time, and his family were converted to Christianity by the missionaries. He went to their schools, and stayed on to become a teacher. Not very much is known about him, except that he married and had three sons, and was a reliable teacher for 10 years.

In 1944 Wang was elected chairman of the Church Council in Wuding, and seven years later he was ordained a pastor in the Church. He became an enthusiastic preacher of Christianity, determined to live like Jesus, even though it was not always easy. The local government held meetings to criticise landowners, and often to build up hatred against foreigners. Although Wang tried to be loyal to the Chinese State, he always refused to take part in these meetings, not wanting to condemn others.

These were the years when the Chinese leader Mao Tse-tung was building up the Communist Party. Mao had grown up in the countryside and seen overworked peasants reduced to poverty, while the landowners were having an easy life. Mao insisted that all the land should belong to the State, and that everyone should work and be given the same rewards. It was a good idea, but proved disastrous. Mao distrusted anyone with an education, such as doctors and teachers. All had to become farmers. When Mao became Chairman of the Communist Party in 1949, he proved to be an incapable leader, and 20 million people starved to death. He punished anyone who criticised him, and missionaries and known Christians were sent to prison.

In Wuding many Christian and Muslim leaders were sent to prison camps or publicly beaten. Wang himself was openly critical of the Mao supporters called Red Guards. In 1969, he was arrested together with members of his family. Four years later he was condemned to death, and executed before a rally of 10,000 people. Today there are still 30,000 Christians in Wuding, and in 1980 the Communist Party pardoned Wang and gave compensation to his family. But what cheered the family most was the knowledge that Wang Zhiming is now honoured as a Christian martyr. Memorials to him have been erected both in Wuding, and on the West Front of Westminster Abbey.

THINK ABOUT IT
Would you be able to speak the truth if it meant suffering?

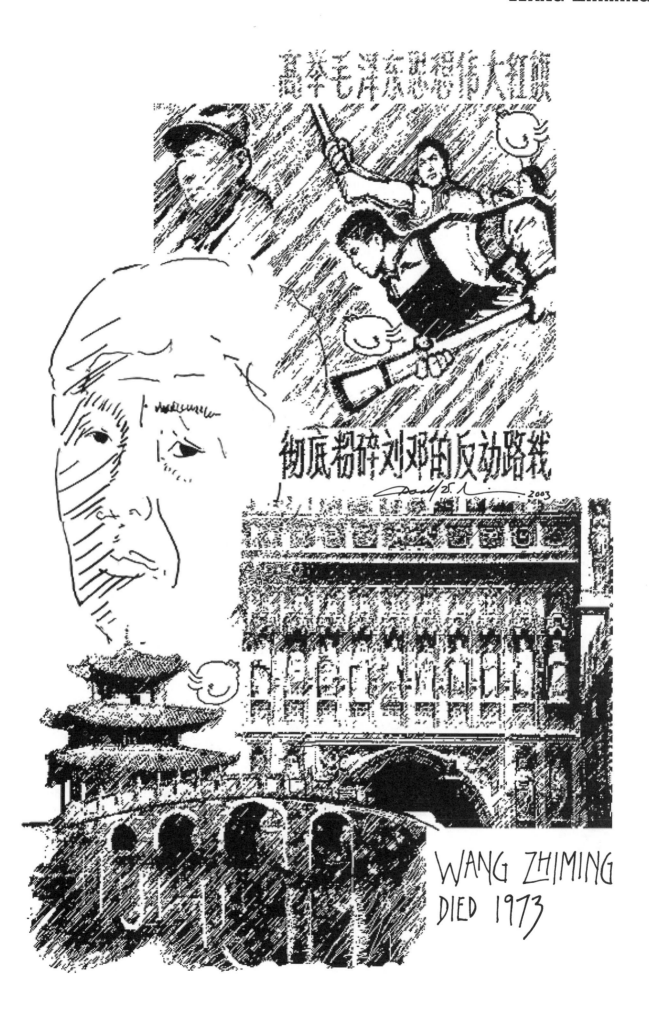

WANG ZHIMING
DIED 1973

WULFSTAN (SAINT)

FEAST DAY: 19 JANUARY

D. 1095

Wulfstan is one of the early English saints who was greatly loved by everyone who knew him. He did some remarkable things in his life, in spite of not being very learned. He may not have been too good at school tests. There are no records of him becoming a theologian (a thinker), or a great teacher. But he was very practical, and was to become a great and respected leader.

Wulfstan was born at the beginning of the eleventh century – the end of Saxon times. His family came from the Midlands, from a village called Long Itchington. He was sent to the abbey schools in Evesham and Peterborough. Before he became a priest, he entered the household of the Bishop of Worcester. When he was ordained a priest, he was offered a very good parish, where he could have lived in comfort. But instead he chose to become a monk at the small Worcester Cathedral priory. There were only 12 monks, and Wulfstan was content to pray and work as one of them. Eventually he became their prior (leader).

What Wulfstan worked at hardest was getting his monks to realise that the Rule of St Benedict was worth following faithfully. They grew to love him because he listened to their needs and their ideas, and because he always worked alongside them. It is not surprising that many young men heard about this happy community, and before long there were 50 monks at Worcester. In 1063 Wulfstan was made the Bishop of Worcester. He wasn't too happy about it, because what he liked most was working humbly in the monastery. But he was a brilliant leader. He was hard-working, and visited every part of his diocese regularly, unlike many other bishops.

During these troublesome times, both England and the Church needed people like Wulfstan. In 1066 William the Conqueror came from Normandy and invaded England. Wulfstan was the first of the bishops to accept Norman rule. He had Benedictine friends in monasteries in Normandy, so he didn't find it as difficult as some others did. He was able to help his people accept the new laws and way of life. He had a number of problems with the barons, and with Welsh soldiers crossing the border, but always managed to keep the peace. He built new churches and persuaded his priests to live better lives. He even rebuilt his cathedral in Worcester.

One of the amazing achievements of Bishop Wulfstan was to stop the slave trade in Bristol. Most people just accepted that transporting slaves to England was a sensible thing to do. Wulfstan saw it as a terrible wrong. Sadly it took another 800 years until the saintly William Wilberforce was able to get slavery totally abolished.

THINK ABOUT IT
Every simple job is **worth doing well**.

WULFSTAN   DIED 1095

FURTHER READING

These are some of the books I referred to when writing these short bigraphies. There are many more that I have come across in school and public libraries.

Donald Attwater, *The Penguin Dictionary of Saints* (Penguin, 1983).

Andrew Chandler, *Christian Martyrs of the Twentieth Century* (the ten new statues on the West Front of Westminster Abbey) (Beric Tempest, 1998).

Joan Chittister, *A Passion for Life* (Orbis Books, 1996).

John Coulson (ed.), *The Saints. A Concise Biographical Dictionary* (Burns & Oates, 1958).

Kathleen Jones, *The Saints of the Anglican Calendar* (Canterbury Press, 2000).

Richard Symonds, *Far Above Rubies* (saintly women in the Anglican Church) (Fowler Wright, 1993).

CTS Biographies Series.